PRAGMATIC WCF

RAHUL SAHAY

Pragmatic WCF

Pragmatic WCF

CONTENTS

Chapter 1: Getting started

CHAPTER 2: CONTRACTS & SERVICES

Pragmatic WCF

Pragmatic WCF

CHAPTER 5: THREADING

CHAPTER 6: BINDINGS & SERVICE BEHAVIOR

Pragmatic WCF

CHAPTER 7: METADATA

CHAPTER 8: INSTANCING & CONCURRENCY

Pragmatic WCF

CHAPTER 9: FAULTS AND EXCEPTIONS

Pragmatic WCF

CHAPTER 10: OPERATION MANAGEMENT

CHAPTER 11: SECURITY

Pragmatic WCF

PREFACE

Hello and welcome to Pragmatic WCF. My entire career has been about learning new technologies and applying the same. It is like taking on new challenges and implementing the same efficiently. I enjoy learning new stuffs, and I like to share things that I have learned through blogging and book writing. I also like to help others by cascading the knowledge related to different technologies. I always wanted to write a book where I can highlight some of the enterprise level coding practice in the field of distributed technology. I also wanted to show something that solved the kinds of problems that architects and developers face on daily basis while writing enterprise level solution. After years of research and hard work, I finally put all the topics with complete demo in place.

There are many reasons why WCF came to my mind. Undoubtedly my focus on web services and interoperability. Given that WCF has deep support for web service standards (WS*) and supports high degree of extensibility. Another quality about WCF that impresses me is that it embraces pure SOA platform, which means decoupling the development of services from downstream business components. In short, WCF unifies earlier technology stacks, namely .NET Remoting, Enterprise Services, ASP.NET web services (ASMX), and Web Services Enhancements (WSE).

I am strong believer of the fact that anyone developing enterprise systems today should be using WCF. Because the kind of tooling support provided by WCF is simply awesome. Another feature about WCF, which I like most, is its explicitness. WCF is an enabler of robust system design, which confirms security, reliability, and scalability.

I wrote this book to demonstrate developers the power of WCF with complete end-to-end illustrations.

Pragmatic WCF

The primary target audience for this book is anyone who would like to explore the world of SOA implementation using WCF. This book starts with basic understanding then moving to advanced section. Any .NET developer novice or expert can use this book as reference. In addition, anyone who is interested in learning how to design decoupled system right from the scratch, I think he/she is at best place.

Chapter 1, Getting Started

Starts by explaining what WCF is, and then describes essential WCF concepts and building blocks of it. The chapter starts with a discussion of the SOA application, which is really the kingpin of all that is enabled in the subsequent chapters. This chapter starts with scratch with basic definitions and comparison with other cousin technologies.

Chapter 2, Contracts & Services

In this chapter, I discussed Contracts and Services in detail. Contracts and Services are the heart of any WCF application. Here, you will start with basic understanding. Then, you will see demos around it with deep understanding around designing contracts and service.

Chapter 3, Hosting

Hosting is the key ingredient to give life to your service. Here, you will learn variety of techniques to host the services. Here, you will also learn how to host the services in different scenarios with different protocols.

Chapter 4, Creating Proxy & Client Configuration

This section is entirely dedicated to proxy creation and consuming service. Here, you will learn while doing so, what are underline factors involved like how channel plays an important role around proxy. Then, you will also learn things like communication establishment, security establishment, message exchange etc...

Chapter 5, Threading

Pragmatic WCF

In this chapter, you will learn how to handle threading issues in real time environment. Here, you will also learn how to keep the UI responsive while operation is executing in the background thread. Major thing is how to delegate the job to different threads while keeping the UI thread free for accepting multiple requests.

Chapter 6, Bindings & Service Behavior

In this chapter, you will learn complete suite of different bindings available with WCF. Binding is one of the key elements for building any WCF application. Here, you will do deep dive with different Transport Mechanisms available for the WCF application.

Chapter 7, Metadata

Metadata is the Shape and Characteristics of service. In short it is pretty much everything about service. All these bits are part of metadata and this is exposed in the form of WSDL. Here, you will learn Metadata Exchange in detail.

Chapter 8, Instancing & Concurrency

Instancing means instance of service whereas concurrency determines how the service will handle locking during multiple concurrent calls. In this Chapter, you will learn two major things Instancing and Concurrency. In the first section, you will learn Instancing and then concurrency.

Chapter 9, Faults & Exceptions

Faults & Exceptions one of the most important pieces of WCF. I have seen that people do not take this section seriously. However, in case of WCF, this is important as we are talking cross boundary here. Therefore, it is important to understand how and when SOAP exceptions occur and how to handle them.

Chapter 10, Operation Management

Demystifies WCF by making operation calls differently. This is one of the unique features of WCF. Unlike Web API, which is again a great technology but it does the operation handling only one-way. Nevertheless, here you will learn different ways.

Chapter 11, Security

Pragmatic WCF

Security is one of the most important areas of any application. More secure you will make your application, more reliable it will be. In this chapter, you will learn different kinds of security implications and their solution. Here, you will also learn how to implement different techniques in intranet and internet scenario.

WHAT IS NOT COVERED

This book is the first part of WCF series where in I have covered major things what developers' need on day-to-day basis. However, there are certain things, which I have not covered in this book like Transaction Handling, Queuing, Routing, Service Bus and many other things. I always feel Transactions go hand in hand with other advanced topic, hence moved this out for next edition.

ACKNOWLEDGEMENTS

Again, this book would not have been possible without the loving support of my wife Nivi, who had to take over much of the household responsibility apart from her teaching activities. Appreciation also goes out to my Mom and Dad for believing in me and always keeps on encouraging me to complete the book in a best possible way. In addition, in the end, you know how it is, you pick a book and flip to Acknowledgement's page and find that author has once again dedicated the book someone close to him, not to you. Not this time. I would like to thank all the readers whole-heartedly for choosing the book. Finally, I would like to thank readers of my blog (http://myview.rahulnivi.net). Many of you have contributed by asking questions, providing feedback, and inspiring and encouraging me in everything, I do.

CHAPTER 1: GETTING STARTED

WHAT DO you find in this CHAPTER?

- Introduction
- What is SOA
- What is Service
- Service Oriented Architecture
- Service Oriented Application

Pragmatic WCF

- Service Oriented Technologies
- Alternative Technologies
- Windows Communication Foundation
- WCF Architecture
- WCF Vs Web API
- Components
- When to consider
- Summary

INTRODUCTION:-

Hello and welcome to Pragmatic WCF. In this section, we will begin with the simple definition and meaning of WCF, and then we will gradually see individual items as explained in the definition. We will also see the different components involved in SOA application and technology behind the scene. Then, we will also compare WCF and Web API and its capabilities. Last but not the least we will also see when to consider WCF. So, without wasting time let us get started.

WHAT IS SOA:-

SOA stands for "**Service Oriented Application**". As per Wikipedia SOA means "A **service-oriented architecture (SOA)** is a design pattern in which application components provide services to other components via a communications protocol, typically over a network. The principles of service-orientation are independent of any vendor, product or technology". Now, let us understand the same in plain English; it is writing a system in such a way that you are exposing everything behind the firewall via some **API** and client has limited functionality access and it accomplishes its job via **Service Calls**. Therefore, it is a way of organizing your system where the client has little intelligence about it and makes the call to access the functionality.

One point to note here in the world of SOA, application's business layer orchestrated by a set of loosely coupled services. Loosely coupled services mean services, which communicate with the client or with each other via set of industry-accepted protocols, in this case SOAP (**Simple Object Access Protocol**).

Pragmatic WCF

WHAT IS SERVICE:-

A Service is a collection of Units of Responsibilities. In WCF, we use the term Operations to define responsibilities. These units of responsibilities are rock solid in handling designated responsibility means anything, which needs orchestrated by making down level calls to other components, is handled by service operation. Let us say if security is necessary then it will handle by service, if some kind of operation mode or concurrency issue or behaviors etc. will be taken care by service itself. Hence, in this case client does not need to worry about these down-level things. Client only need to make a call and that is it. A service itself is a point of entry for the client and sits on the top of this architecture, which we will see soon. Services are also manager of all the down level layers. These down level layers could be business repository or database repository or combination of both. Moreover, because of these reasons, services are secure, keep system healthy, consistent, and thread safe and many other things, which we will discuss in different modules.

SERVICE ORIENTED ARCHITECTURE:-

Everything I described illustrated below in the diagram. As you can see that we have database and data access layer, we have the business layer and we have the UI (Presentation) layer. These are the three basic components of any application, which are required at minimum. Now, when we expose things as services to make our application service oriented, we are hiding away all the calls to the data access layers and business access layer. We are hiding the same using **Firewall** and this **Firewall** in this diagram is termed as **Service Layer**. Because, Service Layer exposed using industry accepted protocol, there is lot of low-level communication need to happen. Here, in this case we are talking between machines means going from one machine to another. Therefore, in order to access services from the client side we use **Service Proxies**. This layer abstracts all low-level communication and setup the connection between client and service. Therefore, all kind of handshaking happens at this layer. In addition, client has no knowledge of all these handshakings.

Pragmatic WCF

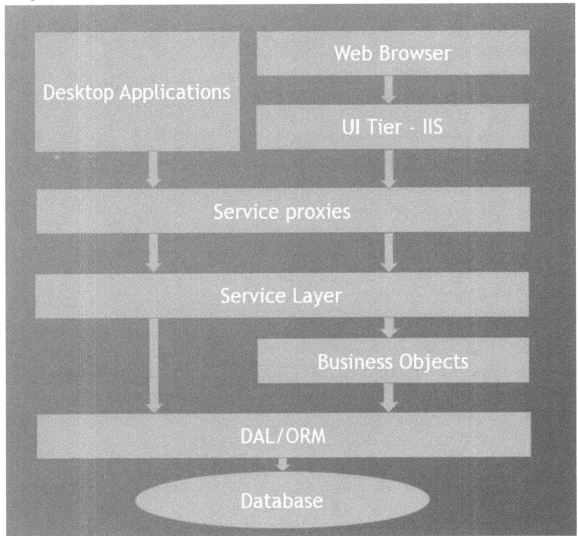

SERVICE ORIENTED APPLICATION:-

An application, which follow above rules, referred as Service Oriented Application. All the SOA applications are whose sensitive areas wrapped inside service call. This is known as operation. However, client not exposed to any of these inner implementations. This hides away anything which client should not have access. It also prevents client from unwanted intrusion into other parts of the system. It also removes potentially dangerous configurations from client machine like connection string. Connection strings could be dangerous thing if not encrypted. Therefore, with SOA applications, clients do not need to bother of these issues; they just need make a service call and all heavy lifting done by service itself.

Pragmatic WCF

In Service Oriented Applications, it is all about the call.

- Client makes a call with required data for processing
- Service receives data, performs job and returns response
- Details of processing completely hidden from the client.

SERVICE ORIENTED TECHNOLOGIES:-

To write Service Oriented Application, we need technologies that enforces certain way of doing things. It also needs to abstract a lot of low level tasks means a lot of work is required for low level tasks. Like different ways of handling

- Communication,
- State Management,
- Transaction,
- Security Implications

Now, this technology also needs to provide necessary tooling both on the server side and on client side. Since, we are using SOAP here; SOAP requires tooling that is the number one difference between **Rest services** and **SOAP** based services. Because of this tooling requirement, WCF comes into picture.

ALTERNATIVE TECHNOLOGIES:-

There are variety of alternative technologies, which we have already used prior to WCF like

- .Net Remoting: - Some of the features of .Net Remoting like TCP-Compatible. Fast but bad part is .Net-to-.Net communication only. It also had many cryptic configurations, which makes developers tough to use.

- Web Services: - This was one of the most widely used technology for communication. Still widely used. Limiting factor with Web Services are they are only HTTP based. Also for advanced features, it requires WS* stack implementations which is again little cryptic to handle.

- Enterprise Services: - This provided advances services to components including things like Security, Transactions etc. However, again it is little difficult to work with this technology as it needed bunch of configurations.

Pragmatic WCF

- MSMQ: - Another great technology which heavily relies on queuing. This technology is still around. It is widely used for reliable messaging and disconnected use. Nevertheless, in order to implement the same, you need to learn another API implementation.

- Sockets: - And then we had Sockets. Good for Point-to-Point communication. However, this is again very much configuration driven and needs a lot of low-level plumbing before launching the same. It relies on things like Packet-Size, port no etc.

WINDOWS COMMUNICATION FOUNDATION:-

One thing, which is common with all these legacy technologies, is that proof of the technology and the communication found in the code, which you write. Therefore, Sockets code is different from what you write for MSMQ. Similarly, Enterprise Library code is different for .Net Remoting or Web Services. Then comes **Windows Communication Foundation**. This provides **Unified Programming Model** for several technologies. This means you can focus on writing your service and how the service is communicated or exposed is done via configuration. WCF is SOAP based but it is REST Capable. WCF also abstracts the details of communication, which means you do not need to know how these down level calls are happening. Hence, you can just focus on your requirement writing business logic in you service code. WCF also gives flexibility in terms of transportation means you write your service code once and you can use any transport medium like TCP, HTTP, and Pipe etc....   Last but not the least WCF provides cool service characteristics which can be handled either declaratively or via program. Below is the list of few Features.

- Security
- State
- Transactions
- Reliability
- etc

WCF ARCHITECTURE:-

Let me give brief snapshot of WCF Architecture. WCF sometimes also referred as interception architecture or pipeline architecture. A pipeline or interception architecture is based on Gang of Four Chain of Responsibility principle. Here, it means it should have two endpoints client and service and whole bunch of stuffs should happen in between. Client packages a message and

Pragmatic WCF

send the same to a service by a proxy call. Now, between this client and service call there are variety of things being done and checked. Some of them are done on the client side of the wire; some of them done on the server side of the wire. We will look all these minute details in the coming sections. Below, is the simple diagram for the same.

Pragmatic WCF

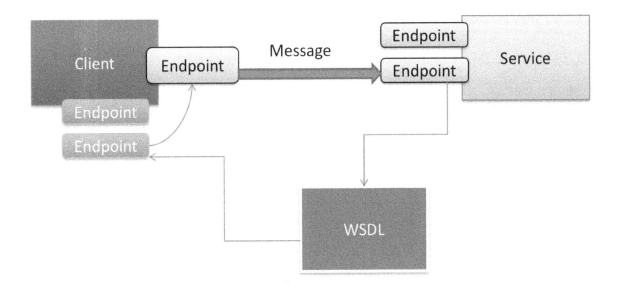

We talked a lot about WCF. Now, let us get rid of that and do comparison between these two.

- WCF is configuration driven and feature rich.
- WEB API is more interoperable.
- WCF based on SOAP protocol.
- WEB API based on REST architecture.
- WCF requires Tooling.
- WEB API requires HTTP request.
- WCF binding makes it faster in Firewall like TCP.
- WEB API is not replacement of WCF.

COMPONENTS:-

In the coming chapters, we will drill down heavily into WCF components. So, let us look briefly, what these components are. WCF is very explicit means you need to know ahead of time what

Pragmatic WCF

you are going to expose and based on that you need to design. In short, WCF is contract based. WCF uses variety of components besides these contracts such as

- Proxies
- Services
- Configuration
- Hosting
- Etc.

WHEN TO CONSIDER-

Most systems today have many client components like Desktop app, Browser, Mobile App, and Mobile Browser. Some of these apps sit inside the Firewall, some out. For example, desktop application sits inside the Firewall app, even the sites hosted on IIS sits inside the firewall. However, mobile apps are different things they are like native apps to the different phone environments like IOS, Windows or Android. Therefore, they sit outside the firewall. However, Mobile browsers are more like mobile simple desktop browsers only difference is these are optimized one, but they still sit inside the firewall. Therefore, the idea is if your application is going to sit inside the Firewall, WCF is definitely a great choice as it certainly offer tons of feature around that.

SUMMARY:-

In this section, we have seen the basics of WCF like the one we started with simple introduction and then looked at the SOA terminology and characteristics of SOA. Then, we have also seen technologies involved behind the implementation of SOA. We also talked in brief about WCF architecture and its role in building SOA. We have also done little comparison with WEB API and in the end; we discussed when to consider WCF for writing your APP.

Pragmatic WCF

CHAPTER 2: CONTRACTS & SERVICES

WHAT DO you find in this CHAPTER?

- Introduction
- What are Contracts
- Data Contracts
- Writing First Data Contract
- Service Contract
- Writing First Service Contract
- Services
- Writing the Service
- Unit Testing
- Summary

INTRODUCTION:-

In this section, we are going to look at Contracts and Services in detail. Contracts and Services are the main essence of WCF as these are basic stuffs, which is going to define your API. Now, in order to do the same I am going to use one case study. My usual Movie Review. Here, in this case I am going to design the API around the same App. In this course, you will see that how I use to fetch movies, directors and many more using WCF implementation.

WHAT ARE CONTRACTS:-

Contracts are parts of WCF explicitness, which means it provides definition and you know in advance, what the things are going to participate when communication happens. Here, in this context, we will be discussing two types of Contracts:-

Pragmatic WCF

- Data Contracts: - Data contracts define the data. They are simple plain classes used to be known as message classes when we used to write web service. These classes have the data, which goes to the service, and response data, which comes out from the service.

- Service Contracts: - Service Contracts define the API. They are the list of operations logically grouped operations exposed to client. This is the only piece, which both client and server share.

DATA CONTRACTS:-

A client makes a call to the service by grouping a bunch of data sending it to the service for further processing and then receiving response. The shape of both the data means incoming and outgoing data defined by data contracts. Incoming data or the request data can be Data Contract or can be argument for example couple of strings or integer packaged together and send in single data contract or that can be sent individually.

However, return data has to be Data Contract, when there is more than one type. Briefly, Data-Contracts are simple classes with just properties in it. Properties we use generally here are auto-implemented property, which I will demo soon. Serializer we use here is Data-Contract Serializer. This is also very much explicit. This is why these are often termed as opt-in serializer. In addition, the attributes, which we will be using here, are

- Data Contract
- Data Member

Before jumping to write my first **DataContract** let me go ahead and explain the project layout. Below, I have pasted the screen shot of my MovieLib solution.

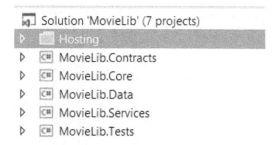

Now, as you can see that it comprise of seven projects. Out of which two sits inside the Hosting Project. Do not worry about that I will explain each individual bits separately. What I am not going to explain here is Core and Data project as both of these projects are part of my

Pragmatic WCF

framework, which I already talked in my earlier book http://amzn.to/1w9sllt. Here, Data project includes data access layer. Data Access Layer uses **DbContext** to talk to dB, which is nothing but **Entity Framework Code First**. Now, if you see the below screen shot my entities sit inside the Entities folder which is mapped to the database behind the scenes.

```
◢  C#  MovieLib.Data
    ▷  🔧  Properties
    ▷  ▪▪  References
    ◢      Entities
        ▷  C#  Movie.cs
        ▷  C#  MovieReview.cs
        ▷  C#  MovieViewModel.cs
    ◢      Repositories
        ▷  C#  MovieRepository.cs
    ◢      Repository Interfaces
        ▷  C□  IMovieRepository.cs
    ◢      SampleData
        ▷  C#  MovieReviewDatabaseInitializer.cs
        🗎  App.config
    ▷  C#  MovieReviewDbContext.cs
        🗎  packages.config
```

Here, I also have Repositories folder where in my Movie Repository sits. You will see me coding there when I make some calls via repository. In addition, for writing testable software each repository is extracted out from its interfaces. However, I do suggest downloading the code from **github** (https://github.com/rahulsahay19/MovieLib-WCF), if you want to code along on the same case study; else, you can make use of WCF concepts directly in your project. This book does not mandate to use my code to code along. You can definitely have your code but you can apply WCF principles from here. The contracts project where I am going to put my data and service contracts. In Services project, I am going to put my services. You need to have services decoupled from contracts; that way you can share the contracts if you are doing referencing. Unit Test project is all about testing WCF Services.

WRITING FIRST DATA CONTRACT:-

In this section, I am going to write my first data contract. This data contract I am going to write in Contracts project as shown below.

Pragmatic WCF

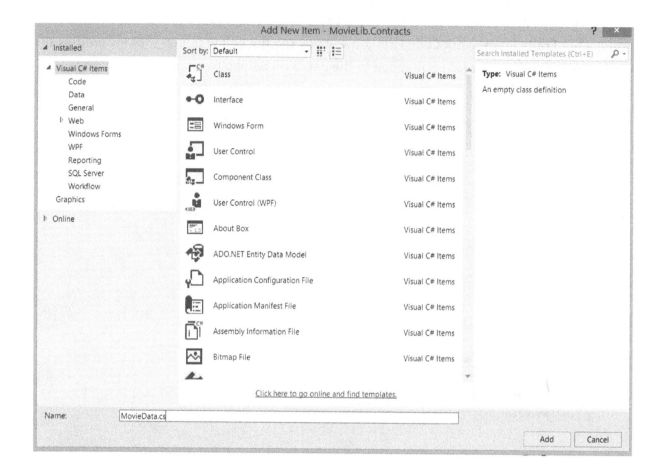

Now, before writing my contract let me explain my entity here. In data project under entities folder I already have Movie class as shown below.

```csharp
using System.Collections.Generic;
using MovieLib.Core;

namespace MovieLib.Data.Entities
{
    public class Movie : IIdentityEntity
```

Pragmatic WCF

```
    {
        public int Id { get; set; }
        public string MovieName { get; set; }
        public string DirectorName { get; set; }
        public string ReleaseYear { get; set; }
        public virtual ICollection<MoviesReview> Reviews { get; set; }


        public int EntityId
        {
            get { return Id; }
            set { Id = value; }
        }
    }
}
```

Now, I may choose to share every information what I have in my entity with my client. However, because of my own reason, I choose to give specific things to client and hence I am putting my contracts in a different folder with subset of above properties. Therefore, as you can see below in the snippet I have taken only three properties, which I am willing to send across the client. One more point to note here is naming convention. In the world of WCF, we usually keep DataContract classes end with the name Data; that is why I kept **MovieData**.

```
using System.Runtime.Serialization;

namespace MovieLib.Contracts
{
    [DataContract]
    public class MovieData
    {
        [DataMember]
        public string MovieName { get; set; }
        [DataMember]
        public string DirectorName { get; set; }
        [DataMember]
        public string ReleaseYear { get; set; }
```

Pragmatic WCF
```
    }

}
```

Now, in order to make it a Data Contract I have annotated the same with the name **[DataContract]**. This comes from the namespace **System.Runtime.Serialization.** If you see the references of this project, you will see two important references and that is

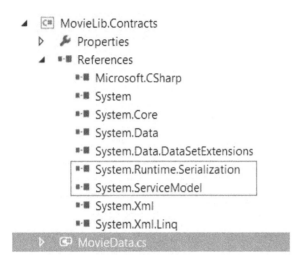

One more point to note here, that everything in WCF world come from the name space **System.ServiceModel**. You might also notice that I have also decorated individual properties with **[DataMember]** attribute and the reason for this is simple. As I said in WCF, we use opt-in serializer, which means until we decorate explicitly, this property will not participate during serialization. However, Microsoft folks in .NET 4.0 change the DataContract serializer where in if you leave out **[DataContract]** attribute from the class, every public member becomes automatically serializable. Nevertheless, I like the idea of explicitness.

SERVICE CONTRACT:-

Service Contracts are nothing but logically grouped operations. A service contract defines the operation of service. It means service contract will be having C# Interfaces, which needs to be implemented in service class. In-fact, a service contract is nothing but an interface with method members only no properties. Like the DataContract, we have attributes here as well. These attributes are-

Pragmatic WCF

- Service Contract
- Operation Contract

These attributes defined in **System.ServiceModel** namespace assembly.

WRITING FIRST SERVICE CONTRACT:-

The first service contract I am going to write is **IMovieService**. This contract I will write in my Contracts project as shown below. As I said, Service Contracts are nothing but C# Interface.

```
◢  C#  MovieLib.Contracts
    ▷  ⚲  Properties
    ▷  ▪▪  References
    ▷  C#  IMovieService.cs
    ▷  C#  MovieData.cs
```

```csharp
using System;
using System.Collections.Generic;
using System.ServiceModel;


namespace MovieLib.Contracts
{
    [ServiceContract]
    public interface IMovieService
    {
        [OperationContract]
        IEnumerable<string> GetDirectorNames();
    }
}
```

Here, in the above snippet I have annotated the interface with **[ServiceContract]** and individual methods as **[OperationContract]**. Again, these annotations are part of WCF explicitness, so that it can participate in WCF Serialization.

Pragmatic WCF

SERVICES:-

Services are simple classes. Services are the implementation of Service Contract for the server side of the wire. Now, a service is the first line of contact or the entry point for the client and it manages all the down level calls. These calls can be anything like simply making a Data-Access layer call and fetching data or making some Business API call for further processing; means could be anything.

WRITING THE SERVICE:-

I am going to write my service in services project and going to name the same **MovieManager**. As I said earlier, services manages all the down level calls, hence I usually prefer ending my service class name with Manager.

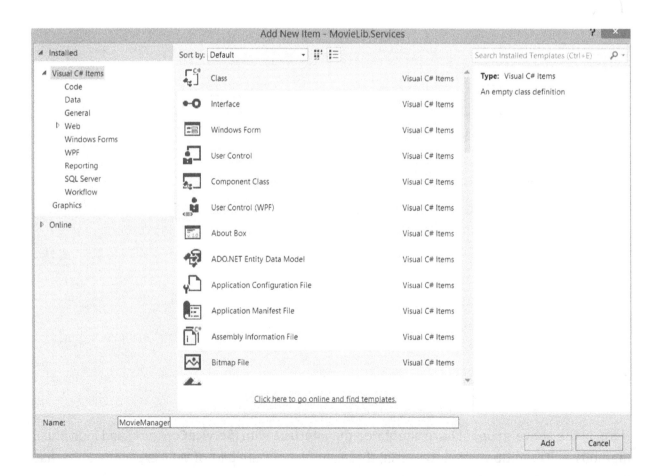

Pragmatic WCF

In addition, not to forget my service project is referencing my all dependent assemblies as shown below in the screen shot.

- ⊿ C# MovieLib.Services
  - ▷ 🔧 Properties
  - ⊿ ▪▪ References
    - ▪▪ EntityFramework
    - ▪▪ EntityFramework.SqlServer
    - ▪▪ Microsoft.CSharp
    - ▪▪ MovieLib.Contracts
    - ▪▪ MovieLib.Core
    - ▪▪ MovieLib.Data
    - ▪▪ System
    - ▪▪ System.ComponentModel.DataAnnotations
    - ▪▪ System.Core
    - ▪▪ System.Data
    - ▪▪ System.Data.DataSetExtensions
    - ▪▪ System.Runtime.Serialization
    - ▪▪ System.ServiceModel
    - ▪▪ System.Xml
    - ▪▪ System.Xml.Linq
  - 🗋 App.config
  - ▷ C# MovieManager.cs
  - 🗋 packages.config

```
using System.Collections;
using System.Collections.Generic;
using System.Linq;
using MovieLib.Contracts;
using MovieLib.Data.Entities;
using MovieLib.Data.Repositories;
using MovieLib.Data.Repository_Interfaces;


namespace MovieLib.Services
{
    public class MovieManager :IMovieService
```

Pragmatic WCF

```csharp
    {
        public IEnumerable<string> GetDirectorNames()
        {
            List<string> movieData = new List<string>();
            IMovieRepository movieRepository = new MovieRepository();


            IEnumerable<Movie> movies = movieRepository.GetMovies();


            if (movies != null)
            {
                foreach (Movie movie in movies)
                {
                    movieData.Add(movie.DirectorName);
                }
            }


            return movieData;
        }
    }
}
```

Now, it is worth time investing seeing from where **GetMovies()** is coming. This is coming from Data project. As I said, Data and Core are prewritten part of framework. Hence, I will not be discussing the same in detail. However, let us have a glimpse of that. First it looks for movie repository where in finds the implementation of **dbcontext** there.

```csharp
using System;
using System.Collections.Generic;
using System.Data.Entity;
using System.Linq;
using System.Linq.Expressions;
using MovieLib.Core;
using MovieLib.Data.Entities;
```

Pragmatic WCF

```
using MovieLib.Data.Repository_Interfaces;


namespace MovieLib.Data.Repositories

{

    public class MovieRepository : DataRepositoryBase<Movie, MovieReviewDbContext>,
IMovieRepository

    {

        protected override DbSet<Movie> DbSet(MovieReviewDbContext entityContext)

        {

            return entityContext.Movies;

        }


        protected override Expression<Func<Movie, bool>>
IdentifierPredicate(MovieReviewDbContext entityContext, int id)

        {

            return (e => e.Id == id);

        }



        public IEnumerable<Movie> GetMovies()

        {

            using (MovieReviewDbContext entityContext = new MovieReviewDbContext())

            {

                return entityContext.Movies.ToList();


            }

        }

    }

}
```

Now, **GetMovies()** is the method defined in the interface **IMovieRepository** as shown below in
the snippet.

Pragmatic WCF

```
using System.Collections.Generic;

using MovieLib.Core;

using MovieLib.Data.Entities;


namespace MovieLib.Data.Repository_Interfaces
{
    public interface IMovieRepository :IDataRepository<Movie>
    {
        IEnumerable<Movie> GetMovies();
    }
}
```

Also, below is the snapshot of the project structure of data project.

```
▲  [C#] MovieLib.Data
    ▷   ⚙ Properties
    ▷   ▪▪ References
    ▷       Entities
    ▲       Repositories
        ▷   C#  MovieRepository.cs
    ▲       Repository Interfaces
        ▷   C#  IMovieRepository.cs
    ▷       SampleData
            ⧉ App.config
    ▷   C#  MovieReviewDbContext.cs
            ⧉ packages.config
```

UNIT TESTING:-

In order to do Unit Test, I need to make service class unit testable. One basic rule of testing is do not instantiate dependency. However, in the current scenario, we will end up instantiating dependency and getting live data for testing which is a bad thing. Now, in order to fix this we need to have a way to inject our repositories. This is where Dependency Injection comes into picture. We can use any of DI container available like Ninject, StructureMap, Unity, etc...But in this case, we will simply achieve DI without any container product. I think this will be good during development for testing the product. Then while finishing the project, we can use any container to achieve the same.

Pragmatic WCF

Now, to achieve the same I need additional constructors. For Unit Test, we can leverage overloaded constructors and put in our own implementation there. Therefore, this means I am going to widen the scope via class wide repository variables and I will only instantiate when this variable is null. So, if Service class used by WCF, then this variable will be NULL, however if the same is called from Unit Test, then it will have the constructor overloads and send mocks. If you are new to mocking I would suggest, please have some basic idea before jumping to write Unit Test. However, in this case I am going to brief about the same. Below, is the snippet of Unit Testable class with additional constructors.

```csharp
using System.Collections;
using System.Collections.Generic;
using System.Linq;
using MovieLib.Contracts;
using MovieLib.Data.Entities;
using MovieLib.Data.Repositories;
using MovieLib.Data.Repository_Interfaces;

namespace MovieLib.Services
{
    public class MovieManager :IMovieService
    {
        private IMovieRepository _iMovieRepository;
        public MovieManager()
        {

        }


        public MovieManager(IMovieRepository iMovieRepository)
        {
            _iMovieRepository = iMovieRepository;
        }
        public IEnumerable<string> GetDirectorNames()
        {
```

Pragmatic WCF

```csharp
            List<string> movieData = new List<string>();
            IMovieRepository movieRepository = _iMovieRepository ?? new
MovieRepository();

            IEnumerable<Movie> movies = movieRepository.GetMovies();

            if (movies != null)
            {
                foreach (Movie movie in movies)
                {
                    movieData.Add(movie.DirectorName);
                }
            }

            return movieData;
        }
    }
}
```

Now, I am going to create a new Unit Test in Test Project as shown below.

```
▲  |C#| MovieLib.Tests
    ▷   🔧 Properties
    ▷   ∎∎ References
    ▷   C# MovieTests.cs
         📄 packages.config
```

Once the same is created, then I will put the below snippet in my test file

```csharp
using System.Collections.Generic;
using System.Linq;
using Microsoft.VisualStudio.TestTools.UnitTesting;
```

Pragmatic WCF

```csharp
using Moq;
using MovieLib.Contracts;
using MovieLib.Data.Entities;
using MovieLib.Data.Repository_Interfaces;
using MovieLib.Services;


namespace MovieLib.Tests
{
    [TestClass]
    public class MovieTests
    {
        [TestMethod]
        public void MovieTest()
        {
            Mock<IMovieRepository> mockMovieRepository = new Mock<IMovieRepository>();

            //Mock return as GetMovies returns the same, so we are not going to hit db
            //we are going to return mocked up entity
            IEnumerable<Movie> movie = new Movie[]
            {
                new Movie()
                {
                    MovieName = "Avatar",
                    DirectorName = "James Cameron",
                    ReleaseYear = "2009"
                },
                new Movie()
                {
                    MovieName = "Titanic",
                    DirectorName = "James Cameron",
                    ReleaseYear = "1997"
                }
            };

            //so, now i am going to setup the mock, Hence below i am telling that when
you are encountering
```

Pragmatic WCF

```
        //following member of mockMovieRepository that receives the following
information of GetMovies
        //obj is the implementation of mockMovieRepository. see, mock is creating the
test class behind
        //the scene.
        mockMovieRepository.Setup(obj => obj.GetMovies()).Returns(movie);


        IMovieService movieService = new MovieManager(mockMovieRepository.Object);


        IEnumerable<string> data = movieService.GetDirectorNames();


        Assert.IsTrue(data.ElementAt(0).Contains("James Cameron"));
    }
  }
}
```

Let me go ahead and explain the code here. Here, I have used **moq-testing** framework for mocking dependency. You can download and install the same via nuget. Once installed successfully, it will show below shown assembly in the references folder.

- ◢ ▣ MovieLib.Tests
  - ▷ 🔧 Properties
  - ◢ ▪▪ References
    - ▪▪ Microsoft.CSharp
    - ▪▪ Microsoft.VisualStudio.QualityTools.UnitTestFramework
    - ▪▪ Moq
    - ▪▪ MovieLib.Contracts
    - ▪▪ MovieLib.Core
    - ▪▪ MovieLib.Data
    - ▪▪ MovieLib.Services
    - ▪▪ System
    - ▪▪ System.Core
    - ▪▪ System.Data
    - ▪▪ System.Data.DataSetExtensions
    - ▪▪ System.Xml
    - ▪▪ System.Xml.Linq
  - ▷ 🗲 MovieTests.cs
  - 🗐 packages.config

Pragmatic WCF

If you see the MovieManager code closely, you will find **MovieManager** is dependent on **MovieRepository**. Therefore, we will mock MovieRepository here. Rather than using MovieRepository which is designed to hit the database, we need to create a test class or test implementation of **IMovie Repository** that has its own **GetMovies()** member and that is instructed to return Movie entity. Then foreach operation will be used to build Movie Entity data.

So, rather than writing explicit test class, I will use Mocking framework which will give me the same test class. In addition, this movie Repository returns me Movie Entity data after hitting the database. Nevertheless, for mocked up version, need to create the mocked up data. Once, mock data is ready, next thing I have done is setup the mock. Here, **obj** is the implementation of mock **MovieRepository** as shown below in the screen shot.

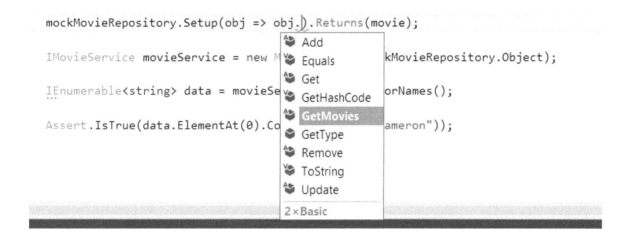

Now, my unit test needs to instantiate the manager class. Once, the instance of the movie manager class is ready I need to call **GetDirectorNames()** which will return the mocked up version of data as constructed above. Once, I build the project and run the test, it will produce me the below result.

Pragmatic WCF

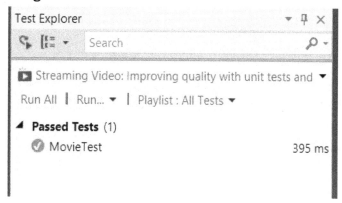

SUMMARY:-

In this section we have get started with Data Contracts and Service Contracts. We have also seen why this explicitness is required in WCF. Then, we have implemented the service contract in the service class. In the first session, we just implemented for the sake of implementation. In the second session, we have used class wide variable to make sure that service is testable. In short, we have injected our dependencies as per call. We have also seen moq framework in action.

Pragmatic WCF

WHAT DO you find in this CHAPTER?

- Introduction
- Self-Hosting
- Console-Hosting
- Service Configuration
- Web-Hosting
- WAS
- Config-Less Hosting
- Windows-Project Setup
- Summary

INTRODUCTION:-

Hosting is the key ingredient to give life to your service. Without a host, service holds no meaning. Host is the application, which is responsible for listening the calls and then instantiating the service. WCF offers two types of hosting; one is called Web-Hosting which is there since web service days. Few artifacts about this is easy to setup, dependency on IIS and only supported protocol is HTTP. There is a catch involved in this. We will cover the same in coming section. Now, another hosting scenario is Self-Hosting. Self-Hosting covers any application. Any application can be host. It requires little bit of coding but gives very deeper control over your hosting. With this, you can setup custom hosting, which will feature rich. So, without wasting time let us get started.

SELF-HOSTING:-

Self-Hosting depends on **ServiceHost** class. Hence, it requires at least one instance of the same, which is in the **System.ServiceModel** namespace and assembly off course. One point to note here that ServiceHost class used in all scenarios including Web-Hosting. Nevertheless, in case of Web-Hosting, IIS instantiates for us. Now, when the host (instance of ServiceHost) is open, it

Pragmatic WCF

requires Endpoint information. Endpoints are nothing but a collection of **Address, Binding and Contract**. We will come to this later. However, Endpoints tell the host how and where to listen for calls from consumer. Now, this information can be provided either from config file or directly from code. We will see that in a moment. Once, host opened successfully, host will be listening and waiting for calls from consumer. Lastly, once opened the host, it needs to be closed as well. Either it can closed gracefully or it can be aborted. Close will wait for any in progress calls and Abort will simply terminate any calls in the pipeline.

CONSOLE-HOSTING:-

In this section, first I am going to cover Console Host, which is nothing but an example of self-host. As you can see in the Hosting folder, I have already created one Console App with the name Console Host.

```
◢  Hosting
   ◢  C#  ConsoleHostApplication
      ▷  Properties
      ▷  References
         App.config
         packages.config
      ▷  C#  Program.cs
```

This is the basic skeleton of any console app. Let me show you the references I have to make the same self-hosted application.

Pragmatic WCF

◢ ■·■ References
   ■·■ EntityFramework
   ■·■ EntityFramework.SqlServer
   ■·■ Microsoft.CSharp
   ■·■ MovieLib.Contracts
   ■·■ MovieLib.Core
   ■·■ MovieLib.Data
   ■·■ MovieLib.Services
   ■·■ System
   ■·■ System.ComponentModel.DataAnnotations
   ■·■ System.Core
   ■·■ System.Data
   ■·■ System.Data.DataSetExtensions
   ■·■ System.Runtime.Serialization
   ■·■ System.ServiceModel
   ■·■ System.Xml
   ■·■ System.Xml.Linq

As you can see in the above screen shot, it has two basic dependencies for any WCF application and it has all the dependencies, which my service is going to need. Moreover, my program class looks like shown below.

```csharp
using System;
using System.ServiceModel;
using MovieLib.Services;

namespace ConsoleHostApplication
{
    class Program
    {
        static void Main(string[] args)
        {
            ServiceHost hostMovieManager = new ServiceHost(typeof(MovieManager));
            hostMovieManager.Open();
            Console.WriteLine("Service Launched,Press Enter to Exit!");
            Console.ReadLine();
            hostMovieManager.Close();
        }
```

Pragmatic WCF

```
    }

}
```

As I said for any self-hosted app we are going to need minimum one instance of ServiceHost; so the very first thing I have instantiated the same with the reference of my **MovieManager** class. Then I have opened the host. As soon as host is opened, it is going to require Endpoint configuration, which I will supply in a moment. Then, at the end of the call, I have just closed the connection gracefully.

SERVICE CONFIGURATION:-

In this section, we will provide Endpoint information via config file. WCF relies heavily on configuration. One point to note here, that anything in configuration can be done procedurally as well, but we will look at the same later. There has been much noise around WCF community regarding WCF configuration. It has been a subject of criticism. In fact, Microsoft in .NET 4.0 has given an option of config-less services. It means that some of the basic stuffs which configuration was providing can be assumed based on other elements. Nevertheless, what I like about configurations is its explicitness and it is very readable. It often gives me an overview of entire WCF system. Hence, I stick to the configuration basics of WCF. In case of config-less, every time any problem happens, you need to dig in code to understand the problem. This is one of the pain points of config-less WCF.

The basic elements of Service Configurations are endpoints. This is the primary thing which host is going to need in order to host the services. Optionally, you can set variety of features to services, which we will cover, in coming section. However, for now Endpoint is ok.

Now, let us go ahead and open the App.Config file. Here, in this file first I have mentioned my SQL Server connection string as it is going to be needed, when host will make the service call.

```
<?xml version="1.0" encoding="utf-8"?>
<configuration>
  <configSections>
```

Pragmatic WCF

```xml
    <!-- For more information on Entity Framework configuration, visit
http://go.microsoft.com/fwlink/?LinkID=237468 -->

    <section name="entityFramework"
type="System.Data.Entity.Internal.ConfigFile.EntityFrameworkSection, EntityFramework,
Version=6.0.0.0, Culture=neutral, PublicKeyToken=b77a5c561934e089"
requirePermission="false" />

  </configSections>

  <startup>

    <supportedRuntime version="v4.0" sku=".NETFramework,Version=v4.5" />

  </startup>

  <entityFramework>

    <defaultConnectionFactory
type="System.Data.Entity.Infrastructure.SqlConnectionFactory, EntityFramework" />

    <providers>

      <provider invariantName="System.Data.SqlClient"
type="System.Data.Entity.SqlServer.SqlProviderServices, EntityFramework.SqlServer" />

    </providers>

  </entityFramework>

  <connectionStrings>

    <add name="MoviesReviewProd" connectionString="Data
Source=8133GTVZ1\SQLEXPRESS;Initial Catalog=MoviesReviewProd;Integrated
Security=SSPI;AttachDBFilename=|DataDirectory|\MoviesReviewProd.mdf"
providerName="System.Data.SqlClient" />

  </connectionStrings>

</configuration>
```

Apart from that I have also installed, Entity Framework here, hence those entries are also present here. Now, I am going to provide my endpoint details. Below in the snippet, I have provided the complete details. Now, if you are wondering that from where, this connection string is coming, so it is coming from the Data project **MovieReviewDbContext** class as shown below.

```csharp
using System.Data.Entity;
using System.Data.Entity.ModelConfiguration.Conventions;
using MovieLib.Data.Entities;
using MovieLib.Data.SampleData;
```

Pragmatic WCF

```csharp
namespace MovieLib.Data
{
    public class MovieReviewDbContext :DbContext
    {


        public MovieReviewDbContext() : base(nameOrConnectionString: "MoviesReviewProd") {
}


        public DbSet<Movie> Movies { get; set; }
        public DbSet<MoviesReview> MovieReviews { get; set; }


        //invoke this to seed default values for the 1st run
        //comment the intializer code in production
        static MovieReviewDbContext()
        {
            Database.SetInitializer(new MovieReviewDatabaseInitializer());
        }


        //setting EF Convetions
        protected override void OnModelCreating(DbModelBuilder modelBuilder)
        {
            //use singular table names
            modelBuilder.Conventions.Remove<PluralizingTableNameConvention>();
            base.OnModelCreating(modelBuilder);
        }
    }
}
```

```xml
<?xml version="1.0" encoding="utf-8"?>
<configuration>
  <configSections>
    <!-- For more information on Entity Framework configuration, visit
http://go.microsoft.com/fwlink/?LinkID=237468 -->
    <section name="entityFramework"
type="System.Data.Entity.Internal.ConfigFile.EntityFrameworkSection, EntityFramework,
```

Pragmatic WCF

```
Version=6.0.0.0, Culture=neutral, PublicKeyToken=b77a5c561934e089"
requirePermission="false" />

  </configSections>

  <startup>

    <supportedRuntime version="v4.0" sku=".NETFramework,Version=v4.5" />

  </startup>

  <entityFramework>

    <defaultConnectionFactory
type="System.Data.Entity.Infrastructure.SqlConnectionFactory, EntityFramework" />

    <providers>

      <provider invariantName="System.Data.SqlClient"
type="System.Data.Entity.SqlServer.SqlProviderServices, EntityFramework.SqlServer" />

    </providers>

  </entityFramework>

  <connectionStrings>

    <add name="MoviesReviewProd" connectionString="Data
Source=8133GTVZ1\SQLEXPRESS;Initial Catalog=MoviesReviewProd;Integrated
Security=SSPI;AttachDBFilename=|DataDirectory|\MoviesReviewProd.mdf"
providerName="System.Data.SqlClient" />

  </connectionStrings>

<system.serviceModel>

  <services>

    <service name="MovieLib.Services.MovieManager">

      <endpoint address="net.tcp://localhost:8010/MovieService"

              binding="netTcpBinding"

              contract="MovieLib.Contracts.IMovieService" />

    </service>

  </services>

</system.serviceModel>

</configuration>
```

Let me explain the code a bit, in WCF configuration, whether it is on client side or server side everything goes inside **<system.serviceModel>** tag. Since, we are hosting here, hence the next tag comes is **<services>**. One point to note here that you need one service tag for every service which you are hosting just like one ServiceHost instance for every service which you are hosting. Then, I have provided the service name and this is fully qualified type name. Now, inside the service tag, you need one or more Endpoint. The service tag is one to one with actual

Pragmatic WCF

service itself means there is one to one relationship between service tag and actual service. The endpoint is at service contract level. Now, endpoints are going to have lot of additional properties, but the most important are

- Address: - The address of the Endpoint is the URL which client can discover it.
- Binding: - The binding is going to define transport medium or communication medium.
- Contract: - The contract is nothing but the service contracts.

These are also called **A, B and C of WCF**. While defining these values you will get some sort of intellisense support to help you incase if you done some typo. Binding here, I have specified is the **netTcpBinding** for a good reason as I am sitting inside the firewall, hence I will pick the one, which is fastest. Later on, I will cover whole suite of different bindings. Nevertheless, for now TCP is fine. Since, I have used **netTcpBinding**, hence, my URL has to be a TCP one as specified in Address. Here, I am done with all kind of configuration. So, if I simply run the same, then it should run fine.

When I run the same for the first time, it will give Firewall popup as shown below in the screen shot.

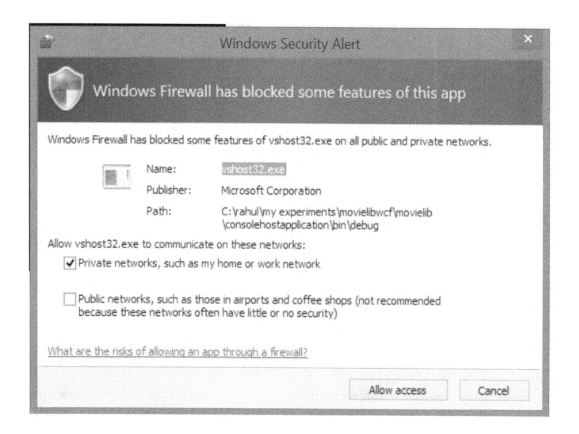

Pragmatic WCF

When, you click on Allow access, it will take you to the output window.

So, here everything is running fine. Now, let us consider if you have done something wrong with the configuration. Let us say wrong URL name, then it would have thrown the exception as shown below.

```
<system.serviceModel>
  <services>
    <service name="MovieLib.Services.MovieManager">
      <endpoint address="http://localhost:8010/MovieService"
                binding="netTcpBinding"
                contract="MovieLib.Contracts.IMovieService" />
    </service>
  </services>
</system.serviceModel>
```

Pragmatic WCF

```
namespace ConsoleHostApplication
{
    0 references
    class Program
    {
        0 references
        static void Main(string[] args)
        {
            ServiceHost hostMovieManager = new ServiceHost(typeof(MovieManager));
            hostMovieManager.Open();
            Console.WriteLine("Servic...
            Console.ReadLine();
            hostMovieManager.Close();
        }
    }
}
```

! ArgumentException was unhandled   ✕

An unhandled exception of type 'System.ArgumentException'
occurred in System.ServiceModel.dll

Additional information: The provided URI scheme 'http' is
invalid; expected 'net.tcp'.

Troubleshooting tips:

Get general help for this exception.

Search for more Help Online...

Exception settings:

☐ Break when this exception type is thrown

Actions:

View Detail...

Copy exception detail to the clipboard

Open exception settings

It gave me the proper exception message at runtime. Here, I have written my first host, which is listening for calls. In coming sections, we will see how to consume the same.

WEB-HOSTING:-

In this section, we will discuss Web Hosting. Now, in case of Web-Hosting IIS is going to all our hosting. It instantiates and manages the ServiceHost instance automatically. One point to note here that IIS is limited to HTTP. Nevertheless, with the use of WAS (Windows Application Services) we can use other bindings as well. Without, WAS we are using IIS for external web services. In WCF, we used to require **.SVC** file for browsing point. However, with .NET 4.0 onwards this need has been eliminated. Now, the same thing can be achieved virtually with configuration itself that we will see in a moment.

Now, as far as WAS is concerned, it requires few salient points.

Pragmatic WCF

- It needs full-blown IIS not express.
- Also requires a modification in applicationhost.config file, which can be done in cmd prompt.
- Then, need to add the bindings in IIS Manager.
- Last but not the least we need to change config file to host another binding.

Let me go ahead and create the web host project in my Hosting Folder.

Pragmatic WCF

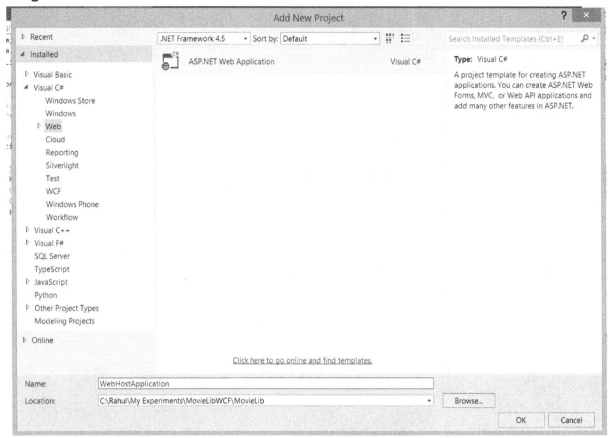

Then I have selected Empty Template from the options provided to me.

Pragmatic WCF

Select a template:

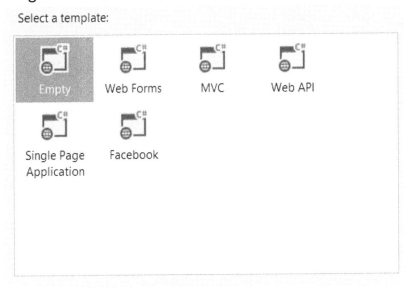

This create me the below skeleton project.

After successful creation, here also I have done the same thing what I have done in console application like adding required references and updating the web.config with connection string and installing the Entity Framework there. Now, let me show the config file in its finished form.

```xml
<?xml version="1.0" encoding="utf-8"?>
<!--
  For more information on how to configure your ASP.NET application, please visit
  http://go.microsoft.com/fwlink/?LinkId=169433
  -->
<configuration>
```

Pragmatic WCF

```
  <configSections>

    <!-- For more information on Entity Framework configuration, visit
http://go.microsoft.com/fwlink/?LinkID=237468 -->

    <section name="entityFramework"
type="System.Data.Entity.Internal.ConfigFile.EntityFrameworkSection, EntityFramework,
Version=6.0.0.0, Culture=neutral, PublicKeyToken=b77a5c561934e089"
requirePermission="false" />

  </configSections>

  <connectionStrings>

    <add name="MoviesReviewProd" connectionString="Data
Source=8133GTVZ1\SQLEXPRESS;Initial Catalog=MoviesReviewProd;Integrated
Security=SSPI;AttachDBFilename=|DataDirectory|\MoviesReviewProd.mdf"
providerName="System.Data.SqlClient" />

  </connectionStrings>

  <system.web>

    <compilation debug="true" targetFramework="4.5" />

    <httpRuntime targetFramework="4.5" />

  </system.web>

  <entityFramework>

    <defaultConnectionFactory
type="System.Data.Entity.Infrastructure.SqlConnectionFactory, EntityFramework" />

    <providers>

      <provider invariantName="System.Data.SqlClient"
type="System.Data.Entity.SqlServer.SqlProviderServices, EntityFramework.SqlServer" />

    </providers>

  </entityFramework>

<system.serviceModel>

  <services>

    <service name="MovieLib.Services.MovieManager">

      <endpoint address=""

              binding="wsHttpBinding"

              contract="MovieLib.Contracts.IMovieService"/>

    </service>

  </services>

<serviceHostingEnvironment>

  <serviceActivations>

    <add service="MovieLib.Services.MovieManager"

          relativeAddress="MovieManager.svc"
```

Pragmatic WCF

```
            factory="WebHostApplication.webHostFactory"/>
    </serviceActivations>
</serviceHostingEnvironment>
</system.serviceModel>
</configuration>
```

Let me explain the config file here. Therefore, inside the service model section there are few things, which we have already discussed. One point to note here, that I have left address unassigned and used http binding. Since, I am going to create the virtual .SVC file which is nothing but my browsing point of Web-Hosting, hence I left address field unassigned. Therefore, the address of this host will be the deployment address itself as shown below in the screen shot.

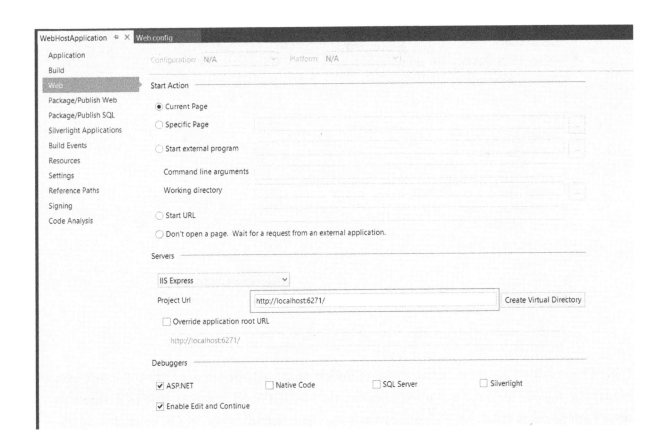

Now, to the above address, it is going to add the .svc file virtually. Initial days, we used to have a physical .svc file. To add the virtual .svc file, first thing which we need to do here is reference

Pragmatic WCF

the **System.ServiceModel.Activation** assembly in the project as shown below in the screen shot.

- ◢ ⬡ **WebHostApplication**
  - ▷ 🔧 Properties
  - ◢ ▪▪ References
    - ▪▪ EntityFramework
    - ▪▪ EntityFramework.SqlServer
    - ▪▪ Microsoft.CSharp
    - ▪▪ MovieLib.Contracts
    - ▪▪ MovieLib.Core
    - ▪▪ MovieLib.Data
    - ▪▪ MovieLib.Services
    - ▪▪ System
    - ▪▪ System.ComponentModel.DataAnnotations
    - ▪▪ System.Configuration
    - ▪▪ System.Core
    - ▪▪ System.Data
    - ▪▪ System.Data.DataSetExtensions
    - ▪▪ System.Drawing
    - ▪▪ System.EnterpriseServices
    - ▪▪ System.Runtime.Serialization
    - ▪▪ System.ServiceModel
    - ▪▪ System.ServiceModel.Activation
    - ▪▪ System.Web
    - ▪▪ System.Web.ApplicationServices
    - ▪▪ System.Web.DynamicData
    - ▪▪ System.Web.Entity
    - ▪▪ System.Web.Extensions
    - ▪▪ System.Web.Services
    - ▪▪ System.Xml
    - ▪▪ System.Xml.Linq

Then, I have added a section **serviceHostingEnvironment** outside services tag and inside service model tag. If I would have been using physical .svc file that need to have name to it. However, since I am having virtual .svc file hence I am using relative address here. As I said, already IIS takes care of instantiating ServiceHost for you for each service you are hosting. Now, a class called ServiceHost factory does this. All it does is receive the type of the service it needs to create a host for; instantiate a service host and return the same to IIS. Now, we can inject custom host factory, which inherits from service host factory. Same thing I have declared in the

Pragmatic WCF

web.config file section. For this I have created, a new class with the name **webHostFactory** is inherited from **ServiceHostFactory**. Below is the snippet for the same.

```csharp
using System;
using System.Collections.Generic;
using System.Linq;
using System.ServiceModel;
using System.ServiceModel.Activation;
using System.Web;

namespace WebHostApplication
{
    public class webHostFactory :ServiceHostFactory
    {
        protected override ServiceHost CreateServiceHost(Type serviceType, Uri[] baseAddresses)
        {
            ServiceHost host = new ServiceHost(serviceType,baseAddresses);

            return host;
        }
    }
}
```

Let me explain the code a bit. Here I have overridden the method **CreateServiceHost**. It takes two parameter; type of the service and base address. Here, I have done the very basic thing created the instance with these two parameters and just returned the host. With this change in place, when I build and run the app, then it will produce me the below output.

Pragmatic WCF

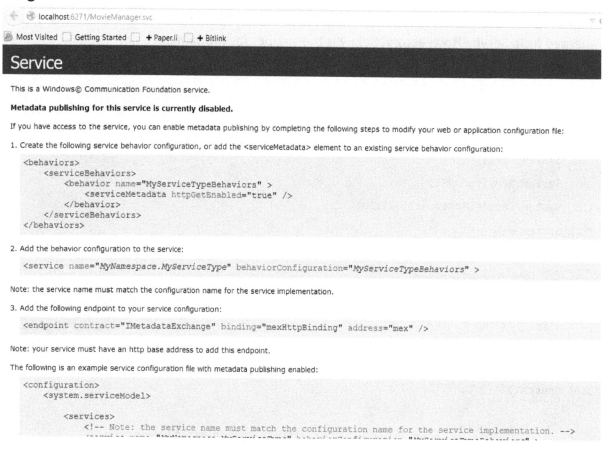

This is a Windows© Communication Foundation service.

Metadata publishing for this service is currently disabled.

If you have access to the service, you can enable metadata publishing by completing the following steps to modify your web or application configuration file:

1. Create the following service behavior configuration, or add the <serviceMetadata> element to an existing service behavior configuration:

```
<behaviors>
    <serviceBehaviors>
        <behavior name="MyServiceTypeBehaviors" >
            <serviceMetadata httpGetEnabled="true" />
        </behavior>
    </serviceBehaviors>
</behaviors>
```

2. Add the behavior configuration to the service:

```
<service name="MyNamespace.MyServiceType" behaviorConfiguration="MyServiceTypeBehaviors" >
```

Note: the service name must match the configuration name for the service implementation.

3. Add the following endpoint to your service configuration:

```
<endpoint contract="IMetadataExchange" binding="mexHttpBinding" address="mex" />
```

Note: your service must have an http base address to add this endpoint.

The following is an example service configuration file with metadata publishing enabled:

```
<configuration>
    <system.serviceModel>

        <services>
            <!-- Note: the service name must match the configuration name for the service implementation. -->
```

WAS:-

My goal here is to use netTcpBinding with this web-hosting. Therefore, if I simply go ahead and change the binding in my web.config file, then it will result me the below error. However, the same can be achieved with the help of WAS.

Server Error in '/' Application.

Could not find a base address that matches scheme net.tcp for the endpoint with binding NetTcpBinding. Registered base address schemes are [http].

Description: An unhandled exception occurred during the execution of the current web request. Please review the stack trace for more information about the error and where it originated in the code.

Exception Details: System.InvalidOperationException: Could not find a base address that matches scheme net.tcp for the endpoint with binding NetTcpBinding. Registered base address schemes are [http].

Source Error:

```
Line 12:         protected override ServiceHost CreateServiceHost(Type serviceType, Uri[] baseAddresses)
Line 13:         {
Line 14:             ServiceHost host = new ServiceHost(serviceType,baseAddresses);
Line 15:
Line 16:             return host;
```

Source File: c:\Rahul\My Experiments\MovieLib\WCF\MovieLib\WebHostApplication\webHostFactory.cs   **Line:** 14

Pragmatic WCF

Now, in order to fix this. I need to do coupe of changes here. First thing, I need to change the property of web host application to IIS.

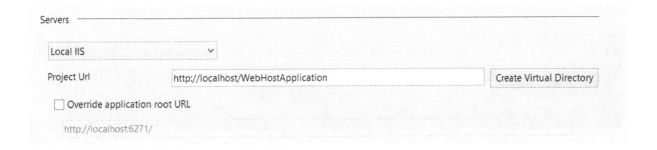

Then I need to click on create virtual directory here. Make sure you are running the project in Admin mode, and then only you can create Virtual Directory from here. Once created successfully, then I need to open the IIS Manager.

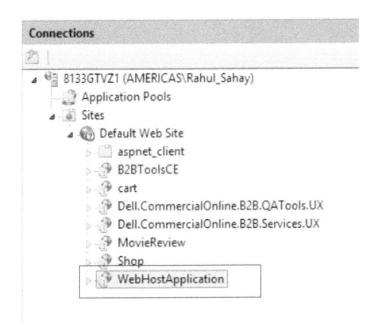

Therefore, it created my application successfully here. Now, to setup WAS as default web site, I need to open up the command prompt and I need to do the same in admin mode. Then, I need

Pragmatic WCF

to go in the **inetsrv** folder and then I need to run the following cmd "**appcmd.exe set site "Default Web Site" -+bindings.[protocol='net.tcp',bindingInformation='808:*']**". I know this command is very cryptic. Nevertheless, this is the one, which I got from MSDN. Therefore, what I have done here is, executing app.cmd executable setting "**Default Web Site**" with netTcp binding. Then, it will give you message that Default website changed.

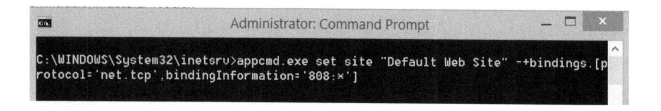

This has modified the applicationhost.config file. Now, I need to go to in IIS manager, and from the advanced setting section, I have added net.tcp as enabled protocol.

Pragmatic WCF

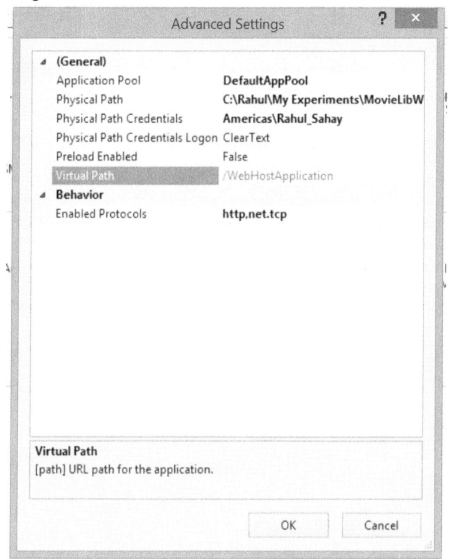

Now, I can go ahead and change the config file as shown below. Here, I have changed the binding.

```
<service name="MovieLib.Services.MovieManager">
     <endpoint address=""
              binding="netTcpBinding"
              contract="MovieLib.Contracts.IMovieService"/>
   </service>
 </services>
```

Pragmatic WCF

Therefore, now my new address will be
net.tcp//localhost/WebHostApplication/MovieManager.svc.

CONFIG-LESS HOSTING:-

WCF does not require config file. It only requires endpoint information. It does not matter which medium it is coming from. You can provide all these information from the code itself. You can get all mandatory information from some source say xml file or database to construct the endpoint. I will give the demo by simply hardcoding the same. Let us go to console hosting. Nevertheless, before making any change in code, let me just comment the config section for WCF in APP.config file. Below is the snippet in the finished state

```csharp
using System;
using System.ServiceModel;
using System.ServiceModel.Channels;
using MovieLib.Contracts;
using MovieLib.Services;

namespace ConsoleHostApplication
{
    class Program
    {
        static void Main(string[] args)
        {
            ServiceHost hostMovieManager = new ServiceHost(typeof(MovieManager));
            string address = "net.tcp://localhost:8010/MovieService";
            Binding binding = new NetTcpBinding();
            Type contract = typeof (IMovieService);

            hostMovieManager.AddServiceEndpoint(contract, binding, address);
            hostMovieManager.Open();
            Console.WriteLine("Service Launched,Press Enter to Exit!");
            Console.ReadLine();
```

Pragmatic WCF

```
            hostMovieManager.Close();

        }

    }

}
```

Let me explain the code a bit. As you can see, I have provided endpoint procedurally. One point to note here is that all of these binding classes inherit from common base class binding. Here, I have created an instance of NetTcpBinding. Then I instantiated a type of my contract. In the end, add I have added endpoint with AddServiceEndpoint method. With the above code change in place, when I build and run the same, it produced the below output.

```
file:///C:/Rahul/My Experiments/MovieLibWCF/MovieLib/ConsoleHostApplicat...
Service Launched,Press Enter to Exit!
```

Similar thing can be achieved with web host as well.

WINDOWS PROJECT SETUP:-

In this section, I am going to setup another project in hosting environment. This will give flexibility to test security, threading, transactions and other WCF features quite easily. So, let us go ahead and WPF application.

Pragmatic WCF

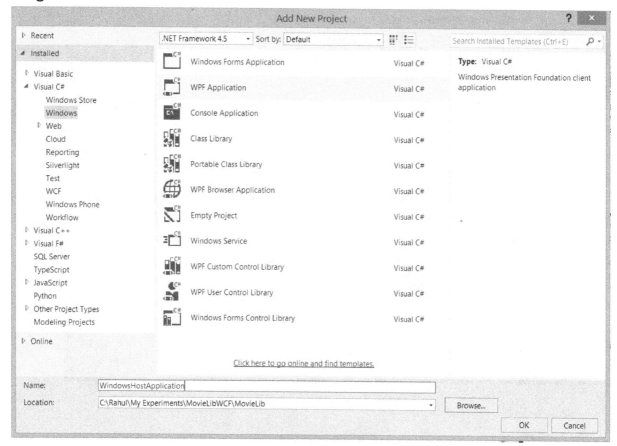

Once, created successfully, it will give me following things.

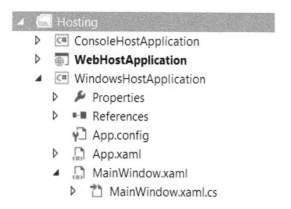

No rocket science. Basic skeleton of simple WPF App. Then, I have done the same basic thing, which I have done with other projects means added required references in there.

Pragmatic WCF

- ◢ [C#] WindowsHostApplication
  - ▷ 🔧 Properties
  - ◢ ▣ References
    - ▪️ Microsoft.CSharp
    - ▪️ MovieLib.Contracts
    - ▪️ MovieLib.Core
    - ▪️ MovieLib.Data
    - ▪️ MovieLib.Services
    - ▪️ PresentationCore
    - ▪️ PresentationFramework
    - ▪️ System
    - ▪️ System.Core
    - ▪️ System.Data
    - ▪️ System.Data.DataSetExtensions
    - ▪️ System.Runtime.Serialization
    - ▪️ System.ServiceModel
    - ▪️ System.Xaml
    - ▪️ System.Xml
    - ▪️ System.Xml.Linq
    - ▪️ WindowsBase
  - 🔧 App.config
  - ▷ App.xaml
  - ◢ MainWindow.xaml
    - ▷ MainWindow.xaml.cs

Now, let us go ahead and modify the form and code behind it. Below I have pasted the code in finished form.

```
using System;
using System.Collections.Generic;
using System.Linq;
using System.ServiceModel;
using System.Text;
using System.Threading.Tasks;
using System.Windows;
using System.Windows.Controls;
using System.Windows.Data;
```

Pragmatic WCF

```csharp
using System.Windows.Documents;

using System.Windows.Input;

using System.Windows.Media;

using System.Windows.Media.Imaging;

using System.Windows.Navigation;

using System.Windows.Shapes;

using MovieLib.Services;


namespace WindowsHostApplication
{
    /// <summary>
    /// Interaction logic for MainWindow.xaml
    /// </summary>
    public partial class MainWindow : Window
    {
        public MainWindow()
        {
            InitializeComponent();
            Btnlaunch.IsEnabled = true;
            BtnStop.IsEnabled = false;
        }


        private ServiceHost _serviceHost = null;
        private void Btnlaunch_Click(object sender, RoutedEventArgs e)
        {
            _serviceHost = new ServiceHost(typeof(MovieManager));
            _serviceHost.Open();
            Btnlaunch.IsEnabled = false;
            BtnStop.IsEnabled = true;


        }


        private void BtnStop_Click(object sender, RoutedEventArgs e)
        {
            _serviceHost.Close();
            Btnlaunch.IsEnabled = true;
```

Pragmatic WCF

```
        BtnStop.IsEnabled = false;

    }

  }

}
```

First thing which I have done here created the instance of service host which is a class scoped variable. Then I have started the same instance in launch button and stopped the same in stop button. Now, it also needs the same config setting what we have used in console app like shown below.

```xml
<?xml version="1.0" encoding="utf-8" ?>
<configuration>
  <configSections>
    <!-- For more information on Entity Framework configuration, visit
http://go.microsoft.com/fwlink/?LinkID=237468 -->
    <section name="entityFramework"
type="System.Data.Entity.Internal.ConfigFile.EntityFrameworkSection, EntityFramework,
Version=6.0.0.0, Culture=neutral, PublicKeyToken=b77a5c561934e089"
requirePermission="false" />
  </configSections>
  <startup>
    <supportedRuntime version="v4.0" sku=".NETFramework,Version=v4.5" />
  </startup>
  <entityFramework>
    <defaultConnectionFactory
type="System.Data.Entity.Infrastructure.SqlConnectionFactory, EntityFramework" />
    <providers>
      <provider invariantName="System.Data.SqlClient"
type="System.Data.Entity.SqlServer.SqlProviderServices, EntityFramework.SqlServer" />
    </providers>
  </entityFramework>
  <connectionStrings>
    <add name="MoviesReviewProd" connectionString="Data
Source=8133GTVZ1\SQLEXPRESS;Initial Catalog=MoviesReviewProd;Integrated
Security=SSPI;AttachDBFilename=|DataDirectory|\MoviesReviewProd.mdf"
providerName="System.Data.SqlClient" />
  </connectionStrings>
```

Pragmatic WCF

```xml
<system.serviceModel>

  <services>

    <service name="MovieLib.Services.MovieManager">

      <endpoint address="net.tcp://localhost:8010/MovieService"
                binding="netTcpBinding"
                contract="MovieLib.Contracts.IMovieService"/>

    </service>

  </services>

</system.serviceModel>

</configuration>
```

With these changes in place, when I go ahead and run the app, this will produce the below output. Off course first time Firewall, ask for permission.

Pragmatic WCF

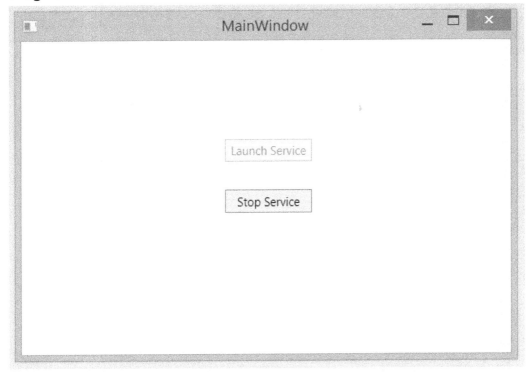

SUMMARY:-

In this section, we have started with very basic hosting that is self-hosting. We have first used console app to host the app. Then, we have used web hosting to achieve the same. In this case, we have used two kinds of hosting first with IIS Express, then with IIS. Going one-step ahead we have also used WAS with IIS in order to host netTcpBinding. Then, we have also explained how to use Config-Less hosting. Last but not the least, we have also setup windows project for future illustrations.

Pragmatic WCF

WHAT DO you find in this CHAPTER?

- Introduction
- Proxy Setup
- Proxy Creation
- Client Configuration
- Inspecting Client App
- Adding Another Endpoint
- Modifying Proxy
- Setting-Up Proxy
- No-Config Coding
- Contract Equivalence
- Creating Another Service
- Proxy Changes
- Service Host Configuration
- Client Configuration
- Channel Factory
- Contract Mismatch
- Version Tolerance
- Summary

INTRODUCTION:-

In this section, we will see how to consume WCF Services. Obviously, proxy classes will be one of the main ingredients for the same. Nevertheless, we will also see how to use channels to achieve the same as well. Therefore, consuming WCF process involves couple of things behind the scenes like communication establishment, security establishment, message exchange etc... Now, these are all very low-level stuff means unmanaged stuff. Therefore, this is the place

Pragmatic WCF

where in WCF Tooling comes into picture. Therefore, with the help of WCF, you really do not need to worry about low-level complexity, as these things will be taken care by WCF.

PROXY SETUP:-

The easiest way to access, a WCF Service from a .NET Client is with a proxy class. Now, WCF provides a base for proxy class as it is wrapper around all the low-level complexities, which I have discussed above. **ClientBase<T>** is the one, which is going to provide this Wrapper. As you can see that **ClientBase** has one generic argument T and this T is going to be the Service Contract, which also means one proxy class per service contract. This also means if you have a service, which is having three different service contracts, then client will be accessing this service by using three different proxy classes. One point to note here that proxy inherits ClientBase<T>, so it not only inherits Service Contract, it also mimic the methods defined in the service contract. Therefore, we have one operation defined by our contract, and then our proxy class will have the same one operation at our disposal in proxy class. Now, in this particular case, my contracts assembly can be shared with client side. As Host requires the endpoint information, similarly proxies also requires the same. This can be supplied either through configuration or via code. Now, let me show the modified project structure.

Pragmatic WCF

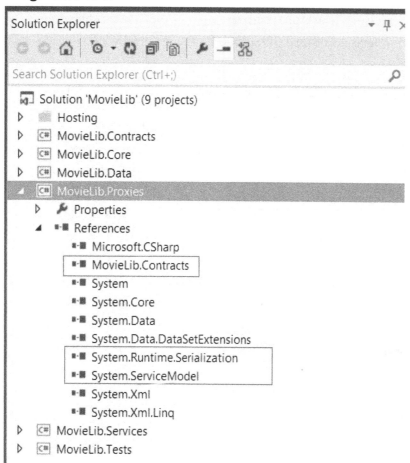

As you can see in the above snapshot, I have added one more project for Proxies, which has the usual references. I only referenced contracts for obvious reason as proxies are meant to deal with contract only.

PROXY CREATION:-

Next, I am going to add my proxy class and I am going to call the MovieClient as shown below in the screen shot. Below, I have pasted the code in the finished form.

```
using System.ServiceModel;
using MovieLib.Contracts;
using System.Collections.Generic;
```

Pragmatic WCF

```
namespace MovieLib.Proxies
{
    public class MovieClient : ClientBase<IMovieService>, IMovieService
    {
        public IEnumerable<string> GetDirectorNames()
        {
            return Channel.GetDirectorNames();
        }
    }
}
```

Let me explain the code a bit. As I said proxy class needs to be inherited from ClientBase<T>, T being the service contract; in this case is IMovieService. Then I implemented IMovieService to get all the methods listed in the contract. Now, when our MovieManager implemented IMovieService, it provided all the functionality of the service. Therefore, we do not need to do the same here. Nevertheless, the idea of inheriting IMovieService is getting the access of Channel property. In addition, because of the generic property of client base, we already have all the methods of service contract at our disposal.

CLIENT CONFIGURATION:-

Before doing client configuration, let me go ahead and add another WPF project, which will serve the purpose my client. Below is the snapshot of my newly created project with required and usual references in there.

Pragmatic WCF

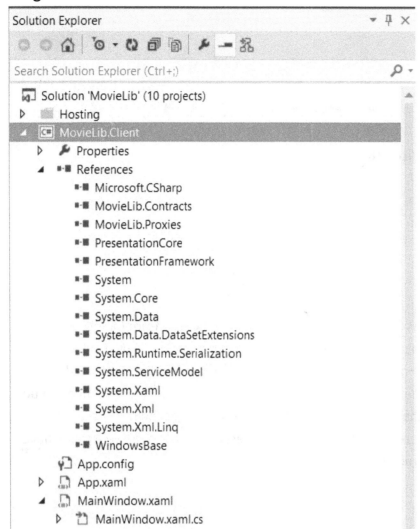

Now, here in the App.Config file, I need to supply all the endpoint informations. Below is the snippet of finished configs file.

```xml
<?xml version="1.0" encoding="utf-8" ?>
<configuration>
    <startup>
        <supportedRuntime version="v4.0" sku=".NETFramework,Version=v4.5" />
    </startup>
  <system.serviceModel>
    <client>
      <endpoint address="net.tcp://localhost:8010/MovieService"
            binding="netTcpBinding"
            contract="MovieLib.Contracts.IMovieService"/>
```

Pragmatic WCF

```
    </client>
  </system.serviceModel>
</configuration>
```

Let me explain the config a bit. Since, we are client here, hence connection strings are not required here, and those things will be taken care by service. In addition, since, we are at the client side here, so instead of **<Services>** tag we used **<Client>** tag. In addition, this is what I like about WCF. It is self-descriptive. Also, one point needs to be understood that Endpoint has to be identical on the both sides of the wire. One point to note here, if we are hosting the same on web host, in that case address would be the deployment address of the web host followed by the .svc filename. Therefore, now we can go ahead and some code in my app to access our service.

INSPECTING CLIENT APP:-

In this section, we are going to add the code to access the service or in short, we are going to place a call so that we can fetch directors. This is what we have added during service setup. Below is the screen shot of UI.

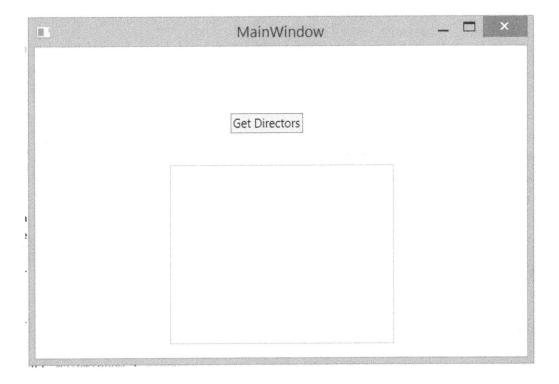

Pragmatic WCF

Therefore, here when user clicks on the Get Directors button, it will return the Director's list from DB. Now, let me show the code for the same.

```xml
<Window x:Class="MovieLib.Client.MainWindow"
        xmlns="http://schemas.microsoft.com/winfx/2006/xaml/presentation"
        xmlns:x="http://schemas.microsoft.com/winfx/2006/xaml"
        Title="MainWindow" Height="350" Width="525">
    <Grid>
        <Button Content="Get Directors" HorizontalAlignment="Left"
VerticalAlignment="Top" Width="75" Margin="203,67,0,0" Click="Button_Click"/>
        <ListBox HorizontalAlignment="Left" Height="180" Margin="140,119,0,0"
VerticalAlignment="Top" Width="232" Name="LstDirectors" FontSize="16">
            <ListBox.ItemTemplate>
                <DataTemplate>
                    <StackPanel Orientation="Horizontal" >
                        <TextBlock Text="{Binding DirectorName}" />
                    </StackPanel>
                </DataTemplate>
            </ListBox.ItemTemplate>
        </ListBox>

    </Grid>
</Window>
```

Above is the simple XAML code for Windows Layout with Button and Listbox. As you can see in the Listbox, that I am binding DirectorName in the TextBlock binding. Therefore, once data returned from the service, this Listbox will list all the director names.

Now, let us see the button code behind code.

```csharp
using System;
using System.Collections.Generic;
using System.Windows;
```

Pragmatic WCF

```csharp
using MovieLib.Contracts;
using MovieLib.Proxies;

namespace MovieLib.Client
{
    /// <summary>
    /// Interaction logic for MainWindow.xaml
    /// </summary>
    public partial class MainWindow : Window
    {
        public MainWindow()
        {
            InitializeComponent();
        }

        private void Button_Click(object sender, RoutedEventArgs e)
        {
            MovieClient proxyclClient = new MovieClient();

            IEnumerable<MovieData> data = proxyclClient.GetDirectorNames();

            if (data != null)
            {
                LstDirectors.ItemsSource = data;

            }

            proxyclClient.Close();
        }

    }
}
```

Pragmatic WCF

As you can see that on the button click, I am creating proxy 1st and then with the proxy client I am making the call, which will go via channel, which we created in the previous section during proxy creation. At the end of the call, it is quite important to close the proxy because as long as proxy is open WCF and client maintain an open Pipe and WCF has threshold limits, which we will be discussing during concurrency. Nevertheless, keeping proxy open may reach threshold concurrency. In addition, I have changed the signature of **GetDirectorNames;** now this will be of return type **IEnumerable<MovieData>** rather than **IEnumerable<string>.** Reason is simple for binding in the Listbox, I need to have property name; in this case it is DirectorName. Hence, I have changed the signature everywhere, wherever it was required. In addition, because of this I have changed the Test Case as well. Below is the modified MovieManager class

```csharp
using System;

using System.Collections;

using System.Collections.Generic;

using System.Linq;

using System.ServiceModel;

using MovieLib.Contracts;

using MovieLib.Data.Entities;

using MovieLib.Data.Repositories;

using MovieLib.Data.Repository_Interfaces;


namespace MovieLib.Services
{
    public class MovieManager : IMovieService
    {
        private IMovieRepository _iMovieRepository;
        public MovieManager()
        {

        }


        public MovieManager(IMovieRepository iMovieRepository)
        {
            _iMovieRepository = iMovieRepository;
```

Pragmatic WCF

```
        }
        public IEnumerable<MovieData> GetDirectorNames()
        {
            List<MovieData> movieData = new List<MovieData>();

            IMovieRepository movieRepository = _iMovieRepository ?? new
MovieRepository();

            IEnumerable<Movie> movies = movieRepository.GetMovies();

            if (movies != null)
            {
                foreach (Movie movie in movies)
                {
                    // movieData.Add(movie.DirectorName);
                    movieData.Add(new MovieData()
                    {
                        DirectorName = movie.DirectorName
                    });
                }
            }

        return movieData;
        }
    }
}
```

One more point to note here is multiple project setting. Here, I need to set multiple project as the startup project; reason being one should be the server and another one should be the client. Now, in order to do the same, right-click on the Solution and add multiple projects as start project as shown below.

Pragmatic WCF

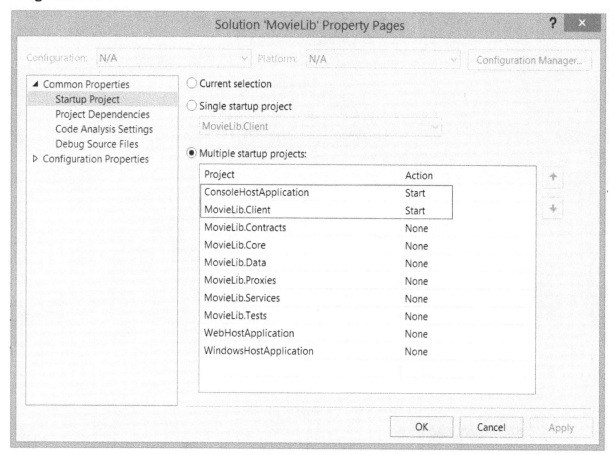

Therefore, with these changes in place, when I build the app run the same, then it will produce me the required result.

Pragmatic WCF

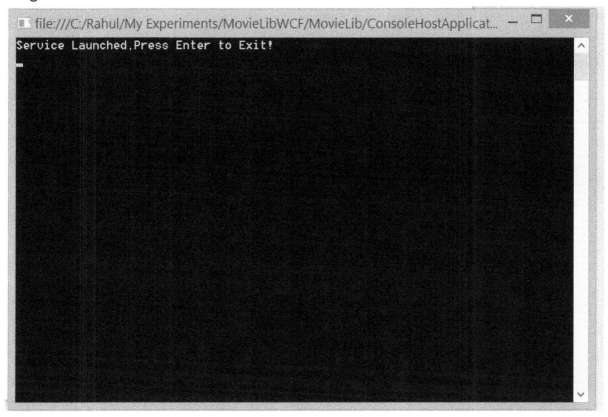

Pragmatic WCF

As you can see in the above screen shot, first window is the one where in Service is hosted and in running stage and second one is the client, which is going to consume the service. Now, when I click on **Get Directors**. It will print the required result as shown below in the screen shot.

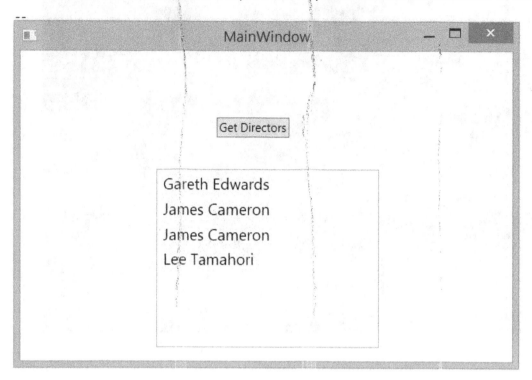

ADDING ANOTHER ENDPOINT:-

In the host section, I have added another Endpoint, this time I have added basicHttpEndpoint. One scenario could be for these extending flexibilities to those end-users who are not sitting inside the firewall. Below is the snippet of host section.

```
<system.serviceModel>
  <services>
    <service name="MovieLib.Services.MovieManager">
      <endpoint address="net.tcp://localhost:8010/MovieService"
               binding="netTcpBinding"
               contract="MovieLib.Contracts.IMovieService" />
      <endpoint address="http://localhost/MovieService"
```

Pragmatic WCF

```
                binding="basicHttpBinding"
                contract="MovieLib.Contracts.IMovieService"/>
    </service>
  </services>
</system.serviceModel>
```

Now, I will copy the same on the client side. Now, there is one catch here. Both the endpoints are having same contract name. Usually what happens when you do not offer name with the endpoint, WCF internally create one based on the contract name and add the same in the dictionary with that Key name. Now, one dictionary cannot have two keys with the same names. Therefore, we need to explicitly give names to these endpoints as shown below.

```
<?xml version="1.0" encoding="utf-8" ?>
<configuration>
  <startup>
    <supportedRuntime version="v4.0" sku=".NETFramework,Version=v4.5" />
  </startup>
  <system.serviceModel>
    <client>
      <endpoint address="net.tcp://localhost:8010/MovieService"
              binding="netTcpBinding"
              contract="MovieLib.Contracts.IMovieService"
              name="1stEP"/>
      <endpoint address="http://localhost/MovieService"
              binding="basicHttpBinding"
              contract="MovieLib.Contracts.IMovieService"
              name="2ndEP"/>
    </client>
  </system.serviceModel>
</configuration>
```

Pragmatic WCF

Next, I need to modify proxy to accommodate these endpoint naming. Therefore, in order to do so, I need to use overloaded constructors. Below is the modified code.

```csharp
using System.ServiceModel;
using MovieLib.Contracts;
using System.Collections.Generic;

namespace MovieLib.Proxies
{
    public class MovieClient : ClientBase<IMovieService>, IMovieService
    {
        public MovieClient(string endpointName):base(endpointName)
        {

        }
        public IEnumerable<MovieData> GetDirectorNames()
        {

            return Channel.GetDirectorNames();
        }
    }
}
```

Let me explain the code a bit. Here, it receives the endpoint name and passes that to the base class, which already has the constructor, setup to receive the endpoint name. Now, since I have modified the proxy, my client code will break.

Pragmatic WCF

```
MovieManager.cs        MovieClient.cs        MainWindow.xaml        MainWindow.xaml.cs  ⊕ ✕
⁂ MovieLib.Client.MainWindow                                    ▾  ⊕ₐ Button_Click(object sender, RoutedEventArg

   5     using MovieLib.Contracts;
   6     using MovieLib.Proxies;
   7
   8    ⊟namespace MovieLib.Client
   9     {
  10    ⊟    /// <summary>
  11         /// Interaction logic for MainWindow.xaml
  12         /// </summary>
          2 references
  13    ⊟    public partial class MainWindow : Window
  14         {
             0 references
  15    ⊟        public MainWindow()
  16             {
  17                 InitializeComponent();
  18             }
  19
             1 reference
  20    ⊟        private void Button_Click(object sender, RoutedEventArgs e)
  21             {
  22                 MovieClient proxyclClient = new MovieClient();
```

```
Error List
▼ ▾  ⊗ 1 Error   ⓘ 0 Warnings   ⓘ 0 Messages
    Description ▾
⊗ 1  'MovieLib.Proxies.MovieClient' does not contain a constructor that takes 0 arguments
```

Therefore, in order to fix the same; in the client call I need to explicitly tell which endpoint I want, and then I can receive the Director's name as shown below.

```
using System;
using System.Collections.Generic;
using System.Windows;

using MovieLib.Contracts;
using MovieLib.Proxies;

namespace MovieLib.Client
{
    /// <summary>
    /// Interaction logic for MainWindow.xaml
    /// </summary>
    public partial class MainWindow : Window
```

Pragmatic WCF

```csharp
    {
        public MainWindow()
        {
            InitializeComponent();
        }

        private void Button_Click(object sender, RoutedEventArgs e)
        {
            MovieClient proxyclClient = new MovieClient("2ndEP");

            IEnumerable<MovieData> data = proxyclClient.GetDirectorNames();

            if (data != null)
            {
                LstDirectors.ItemsSource = data;

            }

            proxyclClient.Close();
        }

    }
}
```

In addition, when I run the same it will produce the same result what we achieved with TCP Endpoint.

Pragmatic WCF

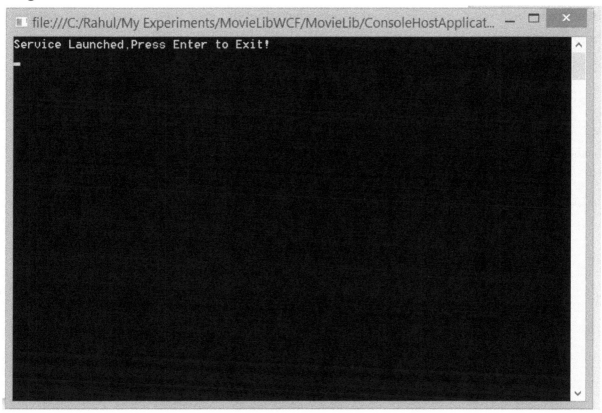

Pragmatic WCF

In addition, if you provide an Endpoint name, which does not exist then in that case, it will give below error message.

```csharp
using System;
using System.Collections.Generic;
using System.Windows;

using MovieLib.Contracts;
using MovieLib.Proxies;

namespace MovieLib.Client
{
    /// <summary>
    /// Interaction logic for MainWindow.xaml
    /// </summary>
    public partial class MainWindow : Window
    {
        public MainWindow()
        {
            InitializeComponent();
        }

        private void Button_Click(object sender, RoutedEventArgs e)
        {
            MovieClient proxyclClient = new MovieClient("1stEP1");

            IEnumerable<MovieData> data = proxyclClient.GetDirectorNames();

            if (data != null)
            {
                LstDirectors.ItemsSource = data;

            }

            proxyclClient.Close();
```

Pragmatic WCF

```
            }


        }

    }
```

```
public class MovieClient : ClientBase<IMovieService>, IMovieService
{
    1 reference
    public MovieClient(string endpointName):base(endpointName)
    {

    }
    5 references | 0 0/1 passing
    public IEnumerable<MovieData> GetDirectorNames()
    {

        return Channel.GetDirectorNames();
    }
}
```

! InvalidOperationException was unhandled ✕

An unhandled exception of type
'System.InvalidOperationException' occurred in
System.ServiceModel.dll

Additional information: Could not find endpoint element
with name '1stEP1' and contract

Troubleshooting tips:

Get general help for this exception.

Search for more Help Online...

Exception settings:

☐ Break when this exception type is thrown

SETTING-UP PROXY:-

In this section, we are going to see Config-Less behavior. Therefore, here we are going to access the Endpoint from the client side but procedurally. Before doing the same. Let me introduce one more button to invoke the same. Hence, now my client will look something like this.

Pragmatic WCF

Now for the proxy to access these Endpoints, it has to pass through via constructor overloading. Below I have pasted the modified proxy code.

```csharp
using System.ServiceModel;
using System.ServiceModel.Channels;
using MovieLib.Contracts;
using System.Collections.Generic;

namespace MovieLib.Proxies
{
    public class MovieClient : ClientBase<IMovieService>, IMovieService
    {
        public MovieClient(string endpointName):base(endpointName)
        {

        }

        public MovieClient(Binding binding,EndpointAddress address):base(binding,address)
```

Pragmatic WCF

```
        {

        }
    public IEnumerable<MovieData> GetDirectorNames()
        {

            return Channel.GetDirectorNames();
        }
    }
}
```

Now, let me explain the code here. As the first constructor overloads the Endpoint name, second constructor overloads Binding and Address name. Here, we have not passed the Contract with the constructor as it is already assigned to the proxy. Therefore, proxy knows the Contract.

NO-CONFIG CODING:-

In the last section, we have done with proxy setup for Config-Less invocation. Now, in this case we need to code for the same but in the client side. Below is the code for the same.

```
private void Button_Click_1(object sender, RoutedEventArgs e)
        {
            EndpointAddress address = new
EndpointAddress("net.tcp://localhost:8010/MovieService");
            Binding binding = new NetTcpBinding();

            MovieClient proxyClient = new MovieClient(binding, address);

            IEnumerable<MovieData> data = proxyClient.GetDirectorNames();

            if (data != null)
            {
```

Pragmatic WCF

```
            LstDirectors.ItemsSource = data;

        }


            proxyClient.Close();

    }
```

No rocket science here. Just the basic stuffs. First have created the instances of address and binding and then assigned the same to the newly created overloaded constructor. After that created the proxy client to invoke the method. Lastly, used the same list box to bind the returned values. Now, when I build and run the same, it will produce me the same output.

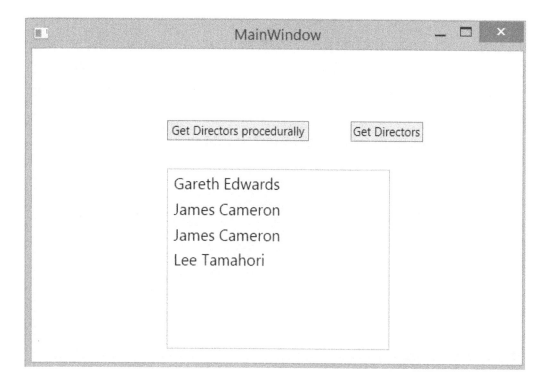

CONTRACT EQUIVALENCE:-

Contracts Equivalence simply means contract names and their operations must be the same. If they are not equivalent as per definition, then you can correct the differences by making use of **Name** property declaration. The declaration can either be Data-Member, Data-Contract, Service

Pragmatic WCF

Contract or Operation Contract attribute. All four of them have this **Name** property. Hence, this is the property; we will use to account for any mismatch in naming. Another thing, which also must match, is namespace. For doing the same we can use namespace attribute on any of above four properties. Now, let us see them in action.

CREATING ANOTHER SERVICE:-

Before jumping directly writing another service, let me show you the Windows Host, which I have used earlier to host the services. Therefore, now what I have done is rather than console host, I have setup Windows Host as the startup project apart from client. Let me the run the same and show once.

Now, I will click on Launch Service button as shown below. So, now the service is hosted.

Pragmatic WCF

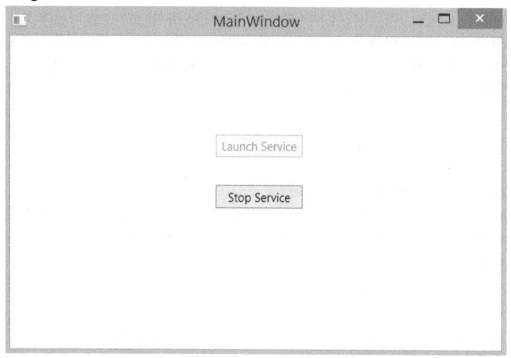

Then, in the app when I click on Get Directors, then it will fetch me the required details as shown.

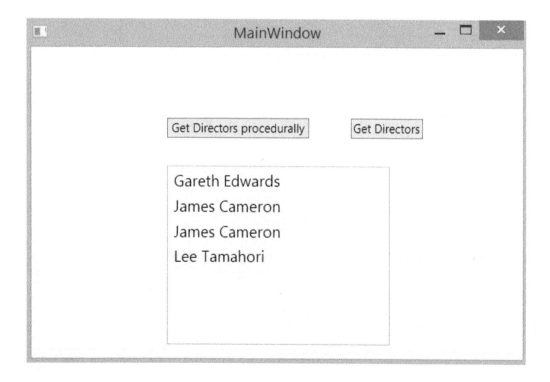

Pragmatic WCF

Straight forward; simple hosting and consuming. So, to demonstrate contract equivalency I am going to write new service contract and new service in the same solution rather than creating another solution which means when my client is going to access the same, it's going to need the service contract. Nevertheless, I am not going to refer the same; however, I will create another replica of the same on the client side. Below, in the windows project I have created one Service Contract for showing selected movie. It simply takes movie name and prints the same.

```csharp
using System.ServiceModel;

namespace WindowsHostApplication.Contracts
{
    [ServiceContract]
    public interface IMovieName
    {
        [OperationContract]
        void SelectedMovie(string moviename);
    }
}
```

Now, I will write service, which will implement this contract. Here is the snippet for the same in the finished form.

```csharp
using WindowsHostApplication.Contracts;

namespace WindowsHostApplication.Services
{
    public class MovieNameManager :IMovieName
    {
        public void SelectedMovie(string moviename)
```

Pragmatic WCF

```
        {
                MainWindow.PrimaryUI.SelectedMovie(moviename);
        }
    }
}
```

Therefore, here it calls the Selected Movie method, which accepts movie name as string. Now, this selected movie is part of **PrimaryUI**, which is again an instance of Main Window as shown below in the snippet.

```csharp
using System;
using System.Collections.Generic;
using System.Linq;
using System.ServiceModel;
using System.Text;
using System.Threading.Tasks;
using System.Windows;
using System.Windows.Controls;
using System.Windows.Data;
using System.Windows.Documents;
using System.Windows.Input;
using System.Windows.Media;
using System.Windows.Media.Imaging;
using System.Windows.Navigation;
using System.Windows.Shapes;
using MovieLib.Services;

namespace WindowsHostApplication
{
    /// <summary>
    /// Interaction logic for MainWindow.xaml
    /// </summary>
```

Pragmatic WCF

```csharp
public partial class MainWindow : Window
{
    public static MainWindow PrimaryUI;
    public MainWindow()
    {
        InitializeComponent();
        Btnlaunch.IsEnabled = true;
        BtnStop.IsEnabled = false;
    }


    private ServiceHost _serviceHost = null;
    private void Btnlaunch_Click(object sender, RoutedEventArgs e)
    {
        _serviceHost = new ServiceHost(typeof(MovieManager));
        _serviceHost.Open();
        Btnlaunch.IsEnabled = false;
        BtnStop.IsEnabled = true;


    }


    private void BtnStop_Click(object sender, RoutedEventArgs e)
    {
        _serviceHost.Close();
        Btnlaunch.IsEnabled = true;
        BtnStop.IsEnabled = false;
    }


    public void SelectedMovie(string moviename)
    {
        lblMovieName.Content = "Selected Movie is:-" + moviename;
    }
}
}
```

Here, in the XAML, I have also introduced one label to show the selected movie name.

Pragmatic WCF

Therefore, now I have MovieName service all setup and Window's Host hosts the same. Here, Contract and Service are in the same project. Now, I cannot access this project from client. I also do not want to reference it. Therefore, I am going to create another copy IMovieName Contract in the Proxies project, which is already referenced by the client project. Below is the snapshot of the project after creating client side contract in proxies' project.

```
◢  |C#| MovieLib.Proxies
    ▷  🔧  Properties
    ▷  ■-■  References
    ▷   C#  IMovieName.cs
    ▷   C#  MovieClient.cs
```

Here is the snippet for the same.

```csharp
using System.ServiceModel;

namespace MovieLib.Client.Contracts
{
    [ServiceContract]
    public interface IMovieName
    {
        [OperationContract]
        void SelectedMovie(string moviename);
    }
}
```

As you can see in the snippet, the contract is the same only namespace is different. Now, this can cause a problem for Contract Equivalency. In order to fix this we are going to use namespace property to service contract as shown below. One point to note that as per WCF standards, the most accepted form of using Namespace property in the form of URLs. So, here uniqueness of URL can be maintained as its on developer's liberty.

Pragmatic WCF

```csharp
using System.ServiceModel;

namespace MovieLib.Client.Contracts
{
    [ServiceContract(Namespace = "http://www.rahulsahay.com/pragmaticwcf")]
    public interface IMovieName
    {
        [OperationContract]
        void SelectedMovie(string moviename);
    }
}
```

Similarly, on Server side.

```csharp
using System.ServiceModel;

namespace WindowsHostApplication.Contracts
{
    [ServiceContract(Namespace = "http://www.rahulsahay.com/pragmaticwcf")]
    public interface IMovieName
    {
        [OperationContract]
        void SelectedMovie(string moviename);
    }
}
```

Therefore, now I have the same namespace from the SOAP standards; even though the namespace from CLR perspective is different.

Pragmatic WCF

SERVICE HOST CONFIGURATION:-

In this section, I am going to add newly created service in the App.Config file in the services section as shown below.

```
<system.serviceModel>
  <services>
    <service name="MovieLib.Services.MovieManager">
      <endpoint address="net.tcp://localhost:8010/MovieService"
                binding="netTcpBinding"
                contract="MovieLib.Contracts.IMovieService" />
      <endpoint address="http://localhost/MovieService"
                binding="basicHttpBinding"
                contract="MovieLib.Contracts.IMovieService"/>
    </service>
    <service name="|
  </services>
</system.serviceMod
</configuration>
```

```
MovieLib.Services.MovieManager
WindowsHostApplication.Services.MovieNameManager
```

As you can see in the snapshot, we are getting the reference of newly created Service. Isn't this awesome? Below is the config code in its finished form.

```
<system.serviceModel>

    <services>

        <service name="MovieLib.Services.MovieManager">

            <endpoint address="net.tcp://localhost:8010/MovieService"

                    binding="netTcpBinding"

                    contract="MovieLib.Contracts.IMovieService" />

            <endpoint address="http://localhost/MovieService"

                    binding="basicHttpBinding"

                    contract="MovieLib.Contracts.IMovieService"/>

        </service>

        <service name="WindowsHostApplication.Services.MovieNameManager">

            <endpoint address="net.tcp://localhost:8010/MovieName"

                    binding="netTcpBinding"

                    contract="WindowsHostApplication.Contracts.IMovieName"/>
```

Pragmatic WCF

```
    </service>
  </services>
</system.serviceModel>
```

Now, it is time to change the code behind.

```
using System;
using System.Collections.Generic;
using System.Linq;
using System.ServiceModel;
using System.Text;
using System.Threading.Tasks;
using System.Windows;
using System.Windows.Controls;
using System.Windows.Data;
using System.Windows.Documents;
using System.Windows.Input;
using System.Windows.Media;
using System.Windows.Media.Imaging;
using System.Windows.Navigation;
using System.Windows.Shapes;
using WindowsHostApplication.Services;
using MovieLib.Services;

namespace WindowsHostApplication
{
    /// <summary>
    /// Interaction logic for MainWindow.xaml
    /// </summary>



    public partial class MainWindow : Window
    {
        public static MainWindow PrimaryUI;
```

Pragmatic WCF

```csharp
public MainWindow()
{

    InitializeComponent();
    Btnlaunch.IsEnabled = true;
    BtnStop.IsEnabled = false;
    PrimaryUI = this;

}


private ServiceHost _serviceHost = null;
private ServiceHost _serviceHostMovieName = null;
private void Btnlaunch_Click(object sender, RoutedEventArgs e)
{

    _serviceHost = new ServiceHost(typeof(MovieManager));
    _serviceHostMovieName = new ServiceHost(typeof(MovieNameManager));

    _serviceHost.Open();
    _serviceHostMovieName.Open();
    Btnlaunch.IsEnabled = false;
    BtnStop.IsEnabled = true;


}


private void BtnStop_Click(object sender, RoutedEventArgs e)
{
    _serviceHost.Close();
    _serviceHostMovieName.Close();
    Btnlaunch.IsEnabled = true;
    BtnStop.IsEnabled = false;
}


public void SelectedMovie(string moviename)
{

    lblMovieName.Content = "Selected Movie is:-" + moviename;

}
    }
}
```

Pragmatic WCF

With above changes in place, I should be able to host the service without any error at least. Let us try that.

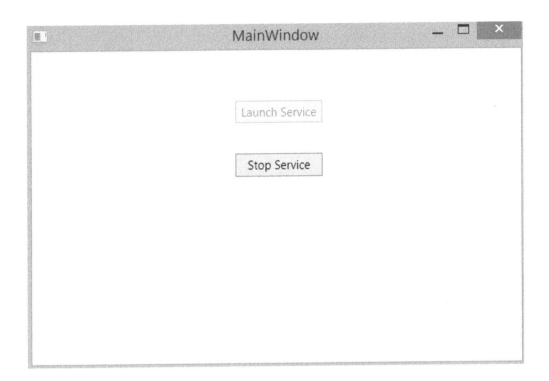

Working fine. Now, let us go ahead and do the client configuration.

CLIENT CONFIGURATION:-

Before going ahead with client configuration. Let me go ahead and modify the UI to respect the changes.

Pragmatic WCF

Then, I'll copy the Endpoint which I have created in Windows Host project and then come in the client config and paste the same as shown below. Only, thing which I need to change in the pasted code is the contract name. Here, I need to include the contract name, which I have created for client side.

```xml
<?xml version="1.0" encoding="utf-8" ?>
<configuration>
  <startup>
    <supportedRuntime version="v4.0" sku=".NETFramework,Version=v4.5" />
  </startup>
  <system.serviceModel>
    <client>
      <endpoint address="net.tcp://localhost:8010/MovieService"
                binding="netTcpBinding"
                contract="MovieLib.Contracts.IMovieService"
```

Pragmatic WCF

```
            name="1stEP"/>
    <endpoint address="http://localhost/MovieService"
            binding="basicHttpBinding"
            contract="MovieLib.Contracts.IMovieService"
            name="2ndEP"/>
    <endpoint address="net.tcp://localhost:8010/MovieName"
            binding="netTcpBinding"
            contract="MovieLib.Client.Contracts.IMovieName"/>


    </client>
  </system.serviceModel>
</configuration>
```

Now, let us go ahead and code the client code. Here, I am going to take a little different approach. Here, I will code the same using Channel Factory.

CHANNEL FACTORY:-

A proxy is a simple class. It is a class, which you can instantiate like a regular class and access its members via object. However, internally proxy creates a channel as we have already seen the usage of channel by calling upon channel property. Proxy is nothing but an implementation of Service Contract. This implementation of service contract can be obtained without actual proxy class rather virtual proxy. This is where Channel Factory comes in. Channel Factory can create a proxy for you and return to you created implementer of service contract without you actually create proxy class explicitly. In addition, channel factory can be accessed both config and config-less fashion. Here, is the code for button click event via channel factory.

```
using System;
using System.Collections.Generic;
using System.ServiceModel;
using System.ServiceModel.Channels;
using System.Windows;
using MovieLib.Client.Contracts;
using MovieLib.Contracts;
```

Pragmatic WCF

```csharp
using MovieLib.Proxies;


namespace MovieLib.Client
{
    /// <summary>
    /// Interaction logic for MainWindow.xaml
    /// </summary>
    public partial class MainWindow : Window
    {
        public MainWindow()
        {
            InitializeComponent();
        }


        private void Button_Click(object sender, RoutedEventArgs e)
        {
            MovieClient proxyClient = new MovieClient("1stEP");

            try
            {
                IEnumerable<MovieData> data = proxyClient.GetDirectorNames();

                if (data != null)
                {
                    LstDirectors.ItemsSource = data;

                }

                proxyClient.Close();
            }
            catch (Exception ex)
            {
                MessageBox.Show("Exception thrown by service." + ex);
            }
        }
```

Pragmatic WCF

```csharp
        private void Button_Click_1(object sender, RoutedEventArgs e)

        {

            EndpointAddress address = new
EndpointAddress("net.tcp://localhost:8010/MovieService");

            Binding binding = new NetTcpBinding();


            MovieClient proxyClient = new MovieClient(binding, address);


            IEnumerable<MovieData> data = proxyClient.GetDirectorNames();


            if (data != null)

            {

                LstDirectors.ItemsSource = data;

            }


            proxyClient.Close();

        }


        private void btnInvoke_Click(object sender, RoutedEventArgs e)

        {

            ChannelFactory<IMovieName> factory = new ChannelFactory<IMovieName>("");

            IMovieName proxyMovieName = factory.CreateChannel();


            proxyMovieName.SelectedMovie(txtMovieName.Text);


            factory.Close();

        }


    }

}
```

Let me explain the code a bit. First, I have created the channel factory with the Client Service Contract. Now, Empty quote here means I am going to refer my only endpoint for the particular contract. If I will be using multiple for the same contract, then in that case I need to provide the name explicitly. However, here I cannot use default constructor without quotes. Therefore,

Pragmatic WCF

quotes are mandatory here. Then, I have obtained channel from this factory. As I said, channel is going to be represented by the implementation of service contract. Therefore, here I have created one virtual proxy class and used the same to print the movie name. In the end, I have closed the factory as we used to close proxy. Therefore, with the above changes in place when I build and run the app, then it will produce me the below output.

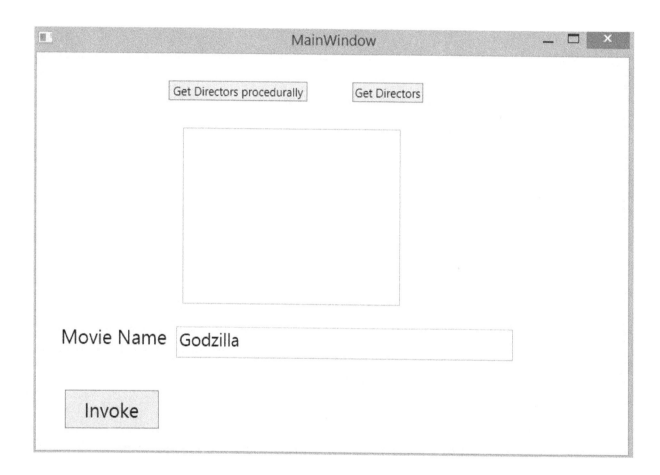

Pragmatic WCF

Above thing achieved via config. Now, the same thing can be achieved configs-less way. Below, I have just tweaked the code for the same.

```
private void btnInvoke_Click(object sender, RoutedEventArgs e)
    {
        EndpointAddress address = new
EndpointAddress("net.tcp://localhost:8011/MovieName");
        Binding binding = new NetTcpBinding();


        ChannelFactory<IMovieName> factory = new ChannelFactory<IMovieName>(binding,
address);


        IMovieName proxy = factory.CreateChannel();


        string value = txtMovieName.Text;
        proxy.SelectedMovie(value);
```

Pragmatic WCF

```
        factory.Close();
    }
```

CONTRACT MISMATCH:-

Here, in this section I will do an equivalency change in the client contract and then show how to correct the same. What I will do here, I will simply go ahead and change the operation name in client Contract as shown below.

```
using System.ServiceModel;

namespace MovieLib.Client.Contracts
{
    [ServiceContract(Namespace = "http://www.rahulsahay.com/pragmaticwcf")]
    public interface IMovieName
    {
        [OperationContract]
        void ShowMovie(string moviename);
    }
}
```

Then, off-course I have to change in the implementation section as well.

```
        private void btnInvoke_Click(object sender, RoutedEventArgs e)
        {
            EndpointAddress address = new
EndpointAddress("net.tcp://localhost:8011/MovieName");
            Binding binding = new NetTcpBinding();

            ChannelFactory<IMovieName> factory = new ChannelFactory<IMovieName>(binding,
address);
```

Pragmatic WCF

```
        IMovieName proxy = factory.CreateChannel();


        string value = txtMovieName.Text;
        proxy.ShowMovie(value);


        factory.Close();
    }
```

Now, when I build the app, it will build fine; but when I run the same, it will throw below error

One easy way to fix this revert the changes. However, there is one more way to fix this by using Name attribute on the operation.

Pragmatic WCF

```csharp
using System.ServiceModel;


namespace MovieLib.Client.Contracts
{
    [ServiceContract(Namespace = "http://www.rahulsahay.com/pragmaticwcf")]
    public interface IMovieName
    {
        [OperationContract(Name = "SelectedMovie")]
        void ShowMovie(string moviename);
    }
}
```

Therefore, from the SOAP perspective this method is **SelectedMovie** equivalent to server side method. At this instant when I build and run the app, then it will produce me the desired result. Nevertheless, using this namespace approach could be tedious when you have many client/server side contracts. We can easily avoid this kind of situation by putting the changes explicitly at two places. One place would be **AssemblyInfo.cs** file on server side and the other one on the client side.

When I open this file it would be something like this

```csharp
using System.Reflection;
using System.Runtime.CompilerServices;
using System.Runtime.InteropServices;


// General Information about an assembly is controlled through the following
```

Pragmatic WCF

```
// set of attributes. Change these attribute values to modify the information
// associated with an assembly.
[assembly: AssemblyTitle("MovieLib.Proxies")]
[assembly: AssemblyDescription("")]
[assembly: AssemblyConfiguration("")]
[assembly: AssemblyCompany("")]
[assembly: AssemblyProduct("MovieLib.Proxies")]
[assembly: AssemblyCopyright("Copyright ©  2015")]
[assembly: AssemblyTrademark("")]
[assembly: AssemblyCulture("")]


// Setting ComVisible to false makes the types in this assembly not visible
// to COM components.  If you need to access a type in this assembly from
// COM, set the ComVisible attribute to true on that type.
[assembly: ComVisible(false)]


// The following GUID is for the ID of the typelib if this project is exposed to COM
[assembly: Guid("32b8859d-fd83-46fc-a990-e8ab0cc1d2a9")]


// Version information for an assembly consists of the following four values:
//
//      Major Version
//      Minor Version
//      Build Number
//      Revision
//
// You can specify all the values or you can default the Build and Revision Numbers
// by using the '*' as shown below:
// [assembly: AssemblyVersion("1.0.*")]
[assembly: AssemblyVersion("1.0.0.0")]
[assembly: AssemblyFileVersion("1.0.0.0")]
```

Here, I will go ahead and add namespace like this. As you can see in the snippet, it takes two parameter 1st is the contract namespace which is nothing but our URL, 2nd is CLR namespace.

Pragmatic WCF

```
[assembly: ContractNamespace("http://www.rahulsahay.com/pragmaticwcf", ClrNamespace =
"MovieLib.Client.Contracts")]
```

Same thing I will copy in the Host project with one change as shown below. So, with these changes in place I can remove explicit namespace from the interfaces and everything will work fine.

VERSION TOLERANCE:-

Version Tolerance is one of the cool features provided by the Data-Contract Serializer. This is one of the things, which is not provided by XML Serializer. One point to note here that Data-Contract is version tolerant up to a certain point. Therefore, there could be a situation that one contract is missing a property means let us say the one on the server is missing one property and the one on the client is running with an extra property. Here, client will make a call by filling up three properties and goes to the service and when service receives this call; it does not break. It simply throws away the extra one. Therefore, this kind of fix you will get by default from Data-Contract Serializer. Similarly, when service is returning the response to the client then in that case it will return with two properties filled with data and the extra one will be returned blank if its string type or zero if its integer type means default value based on the type. Now, due to this kind of situation, client will lose the data.

To fix this kind of problem, we use **IExtensibleDataObject** Interface. Here, all we need to do is to implement this interface in the Data-Contract. This also means WCF will use this an additional container for holding any extra values coming in. So, all we need is the below shown implementation. This will handle all the missing values.

```
using System.Runtime.Serialization;

namespace MovieLib.Contracts
{
    [DataContract(Namespace = "http://www.rahulsahay.com/pragmaticwcf")]
    public class MovieData :IExtensibleDataObject
    {
```

Pragmatic WCF

```
        [DataMember]
        public string MovieName { get; set; }
        [DataMember]
        public string DirectorName { get; set; }
        [DataMember]
        public string ReleaseYear { get; set; }


        public ExtensionDataObject ExtensionData
        {
            get; set;
        }
    }
}
```

SUMMARY:-

In this section, we have seen tons of proxy and client configuration related stuffs. We started this chapter with basics of proxy and then proxy creation. Then, we have configured the client to access the proxy. We have also seen how to tackle multiple endpoints with the proxy. Then, we have seen how to achieve the same with and without config. We have also discussed channel factories and its usage. In the end, we have seen how to handle contract equivalency no of ways and how to use version tolerance.

Pragmatic WCF

WHAT DO you find in this CHAPTER?

- Introduction
- In-Process Threading
- Implementing In-Process
- Threads
- Service Behavior
- Using Synchronization Context
- Marshalling Up
- Service Integration
- Summary

INTRODUCTION:-

In the previous section, I have shown how to use Contract Equivalency. During demonstration, I have shown how to update the UI back by taking message from the client. This call took place from the client from a conventional WCF client means out of the process call. In plain English out of process, call means, client sitting on one machine and server on another and then making request. In that course, we did not run into threading issues, as UI of the host was not busy at that time. Now, in this section, I am going to show couple of threading options and problem associated with the same.

IN-PROCESS THREADING:-

In simple words, In-Process Threading is the process where in your client and host both sits in the same project. Hence, in this case we will be using our usual windows hosting project. However, before using the same, let me go ahead and make some UI changes to it. Below is the screen shot for the same.

Pragmatic WCF

Now, in this the new button will do the same thing what initially client project was doing. When, I press the button it will send the message to host; but problem is when the host receives the message it has to print the same on the UI, but now UI is busy. Because UI is still under the control of button click, which is not, finished yet. In this particular scenario, you will land in a deadlock situation. So, this kind of problem we will solve in this section.

IMPLEMENTING IN-PROCESS:-

In this section, I am going to modify the binding a bit and the reason is straight forward. Since, we are only talking about one machine (Windows Host in this case), hence **namedPipe** makes sense as it is faster than TCP. In short, this is the fastest binding. Below, is the modified app.config for the same.

```
<?xml version="1.0" encoding="utf-8"?>
<configuration>
  <configSections>
    <!-- For more information on Entity Framework configuration, visit
http://go.microsoft.com/fwlink/?LinkID=237468 -->
```

Pragmatic WCF

```xml
    <section name="entityFramework"
type="System.Data.Entity.Internal.ConfigFile.EntityFrameworkSection, EntityFramework,
Version=6.0.0.0, Culture=neutral, PublicKeyToken=b77a5c561934e089"
requirePermission="false" />

  </configSections>

  <startup>

    <supportedRuntime version="v4.0" sku=".NETFramework,Version=v4.5" />

  </startup>

  <entityFramework>

    <defaultConnectionFactory
type="System.Data.Entity.Infrastructure.SqlConnectionFactory, EntityFramework" />

    <providers>

      <provider invariantName="System.Data.SqlClient"
type="System.Data.Entity.SqlServer.SqlProviderServices, EntityFramework.SqlServer" />

    </providers>

  </entityFramework>

  <connectionStrings>

    <add name="MoviesReviewProd" connectionString="Data
Source=8133GTVZ1\SQLEXPRESS;Initial Catalog=MoviesReviewProd1;Integrated
Security=True;AttachDBFilename=|DataDirectory|\MoviesReviewProd.mdf;"
providerName="System.Data.SqlClient" />

  </connectionStrings>

  <system.serviceModel>

    <services>

      <service name="MovieLib.Services.MovieManager">

        <endpoint address="net.tcp://localhost:8010/MovieService"

                  binding="netTcpBinding"

                  contract="MovieLib.Contracts.IMovieService" />

        <endpoint address="http://localhost/MovieService"

                  binding="basicHttpBinding"

                  contract="MovieLib.Contracts.IMovieService"/>

      </service>

      <service name="WindowsHostApplication.Services.MovieNameManager">

        <endpoint address="net.pipe://localhost/MovieName"

                  binding="netNamedPipeBinding"

                  contract="WindowsHostApplication.Contracts.IMovieName"/>

      </service>

    </services>
```

Pragmatic WCF

```
  </system.serviceModel>
</configuration>
```

Now, let us test the change whether existing thing is working or not.

Therefore, it is working as services are hosted successfully.

Now, let us go ahead and write button click event. Nevertheless, before that let me modify the config file to support the client section as well. Below is the snippet in finished form.

```
<system.serviceModel>
    <services>
      <service name="MovieLib.Services.MovieManager">
        <endpoint address="net.tcp://localhost:8010/MovieService"
                binding="netTcpBinding"
                contract="MovieLib.Contracts.IMovieService" />
        <endpoint address="http://localhost/MovieService"
```

Pragmatic WCF

```xml
                binding="basicHttpBinding"
                contract="MovieLib.Contracts.IMovieService"/>
    </service>
    <service name="WindowsHostApplication.Services.MovieNameManager">
      <endpoint address="net.pipe://localhost/MovieName"
                binding="netNamedPipeBinding"
                contract="WindowsHostApplication.Contracts.IMovieName"/>
    </service>
  </services>
  <client>
    <endpoint address="net.pipe://localhost/MovieName"
                binding="netNamedPipeBinding"
                contract="WindowsHostApplication.Contracts.IMovieName"/>
  </client>
</system.serviceModel>
```

With this change in place, client and service are exactly same and sitting in the same application. Now, let us go back to the code do the below mentioned things.

```csharp
private void BtnInProc_Click(object sender, RoutedEventArgs e)
    {
        ChannelFactory<IMovieName> factory = new ChannelFactory<IMovieName>("");

        IMovieName proxy = factory.CreateChannel();

        proxy.SelectedMovie("Top Gun from In Process invoked at"+DateTime.Now);

        factory.Close();
    }
```

Let me explain the code briefly. However, it is not required as you already experienced it earlier. First thing I have done is instantiated the channel factory. Then I have created proxy class with the same. In the end, I have just made the call and then closed the factory. One more thing I have done here; I have added the timestamp just to show the distinction between the

Pragmatic WCF

calls. With the above changes in place, when I run the app, then it will produce me the below output.

Notice in the screen shot, after launching service when I clicked on Launch In-Proc button, it remained in Blue, which means it is still running, hence complete UI freeze and we landed in a deadlock situation. Moreover, because of this we got a timeout error.

Pragmatic WCF

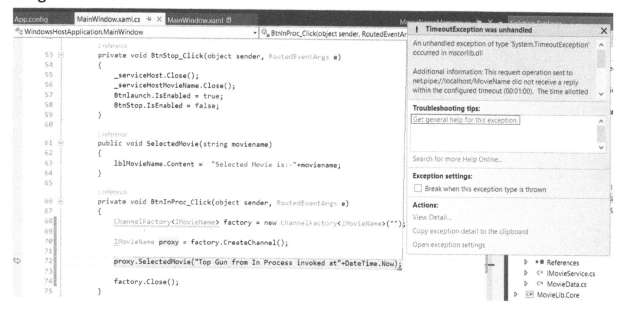

One good thing about WCF is nothing is permanent like we landed in a deadlock situation and that deadlock was automatically released after default time with an error message. Now, let us fix this problem.

THREADS:-

In the previous section, we landed in a deadlock situation as service is hosted on UI thread and a Service running on UI wanted to update the UI itself. Hence, the thread was busy. Now, the key to solve this problem not to keep UI thread busy. Moreover, one way to achieve this by making sure that service will run on worker thread and keep UI thread free for any operations. As soon as we implement this pattern, we will land in another problem. That I will show you in a moment and way to overcome this problem.

SERVICE BEHAVIOR:-

In order to achieve the same I am going to use service behavior. Here, in the Service Behavior, I will set one property **UseSynchronizationContext** to false. Now, synchronization context is nothing but the execution context of any process that is going on and hence every window has it. Moreover, by default, this property is set to true in Service Behavior, which means services

Pragmatic WCF

will execute on the execution context of the host. However, by setting the same to false, I am instructing to execute the service on the worker thread not on the current context. Below is the change for the same.

```csharp
using System.ServiceModel;
using WindowsHostApplication.Contracts;

namespace WindowsHostApplication.Services
{
    [ServiceBehavior(UseSynchronizationContext = false)]
    public class MovieNameManager :IMovieName
    {
        public void SelectedMovie(string moviename)
        {
            MainWindow.PrimaryUI.SelectedMovie(moviename);
        }
    }
}
```

Now, let us go ahead and try running again. Nevertheless, I see one generic error message, which is telling to enable the fault message so that you can see the exact details.

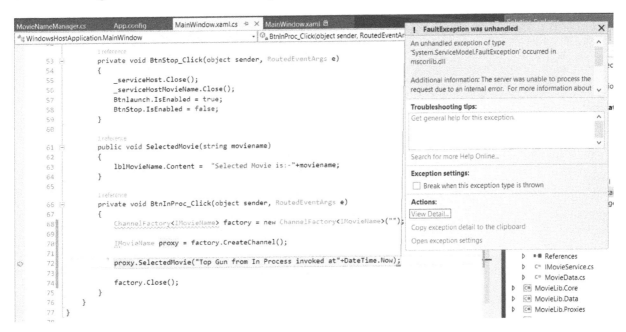

Pragmatic WCF

We will cover exception handling in a different segment. However, for now just enable this property from the service behavior itself as shown below.

```csharp
using System.ServiceModel;
using WindowsHostApplication.Contracts;

namespace WindowsHostApplication.Services
{
    [ServiceBehavior(UseSynchronizationContext = false,IncludeExceptionDetailInFaults =
true)]
    public class MovieNameManager :IMovieName
    {
        public void SelectedMovie(string moviename)
        {
            MainWindow.PrimaryUI.SelectedMovie(moviename);
        }
    }
}
```

Pragmatic WCF

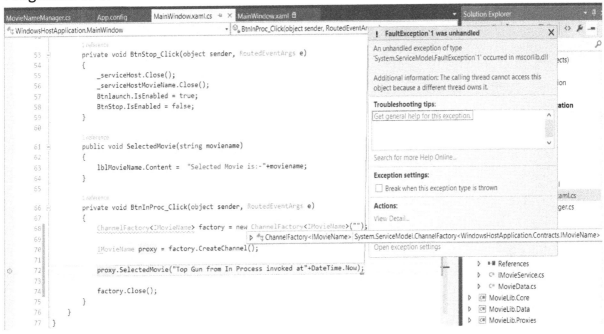

Now, here it came the very famous .Net error, which says, "**Calling Thread cannot access this object as different thread owns it.**"

MARSHALLING UP:-

In this section, we will marshal up the code, which is accessing the background code. To do the same, we will again use the same property Synchronization Context. Below, is the fix in finished form.

```csharp
using System;
using System.Diagnostics;
using System.ServiceModel;
using System.Threading;
using System.Windows;
using WindowsHostApplication.Contracts;
using WindowsHostApplication.Services;
using MovieLib.Services;


namespace WindowsHostApplication
```

Pragmatic WCF

```csharp
{
    /// <summary>
    /// Interaction logic for MainWindow.xaml
    /// </summary>


    public partial class MainWindow : Window
    {
        public static MainWindow PrimaryUI;
        public MainWindow()
        {
            InitializeComponent();
            Btnlaunch.IsEnabled = true;
            BtnStop.IsEnabled = false;


            PrimaryUI = this;
            this.Title = "UI Thread " + Thread.CurrentThread.ManagedThreadId +
                " & Process " + Process.GetCurrentProcess().Id.ToString();


            _synchronizationContext = SynchronizationContext.Current;
        }


        private ServiceHost _serviceHost = null;
        private ServiceHost _serviceHostMovieName = null;
        private SynchronizationContext _synchronizationContext = null;
        private void Btnlaunch_Click(object sender, RoutedEventArgs e)
        {
            _serviceHost = new ServiceHost(typeof(MovieManager));
            _serviceHostMovieName = new ServiceHost(typeof(MovieNameManager));


            _serviceHost.Open();
            _serviceHostMovieName.Open();
            Btnlaunch.IsEnabled = false;
            BtnStop.IsEnabled = true;


        }
```

Pragmatic WCF

```csharp
private void BtnStop_Click(object sender, RoutedEventArgs e)
{
    _serviceHost.Close();
    _serviceHostMovieName.Close();
    Btnlaunch.IsEnabled = true;
    BtnStop.IsEnabled = false;
}


public void SelectedMovie(string moviename)
{
    int threadId = Thread.CurrentThread.ManagedThreadId;


    SendOrPostCallback sendOrPostCallback = (s =>
    {
        lblMovieName.Content =  moviename +Environment.NewLine+
            "coming from thread: " +threadId+ " to thread: " +
            Thread.CurrentThread.ManagedThreadId.ToString() +" Process: "+
Process.GetCurrentProcess().Id.ToString();
    });
    _synchronizationContext.Send(sendOrPostCallback, null);
}


private void BtnInProc_Click(object sender, RoutedEventArgs e)
{
    Thread thread = new Thread(() =>
    {
        ChannelFactory<IMovieName> factory = new ChannelFactory<IMovieName>("");


        IMovieName proxy = factory.CreateChannel();


        proxy.SelectedMovie(
            "Top Gun came at: " +
                DateTime.Now);
        factory.Close();
```

Pragmatic WCF

```
        });

        thread.IsBackground = true;
        thread.Start();
    }
  }
}
```

Here, I have created a class scoped variable of type Synchronization Context 1st. Now, the idea behind synchronization context is to use the same at right time. It represents the execution thread. So, 1st place I have set the same in the UI constructor. Therefore, this will not change. Then in the implementation; I have used under the lambda implementation as a callback. After that, I have set the context again with state null. Then, I have also wrapped the button click event in a background thread just to make sure it will not interlock with other. Since, I have made its background thread, so it has automatically become low priority thread. I have also changed message a bit to show the thread it is running on.

Now, with this change in place, when I run the same, it will produce me the below output.

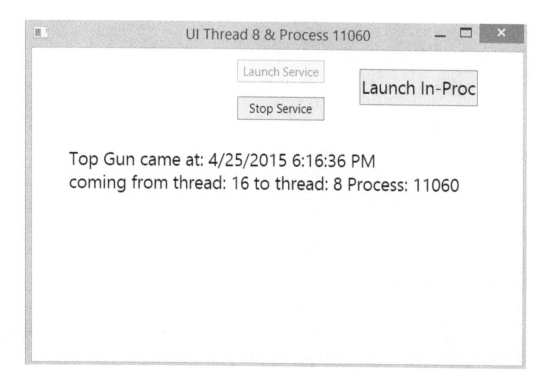

Pragmatic WCF

Here, you will notice couple of things like UI Thread and Process remains the same only background thread is changing, whenever I am clicking on Launch In-Proc button. In addition, button is not freezing like last time.

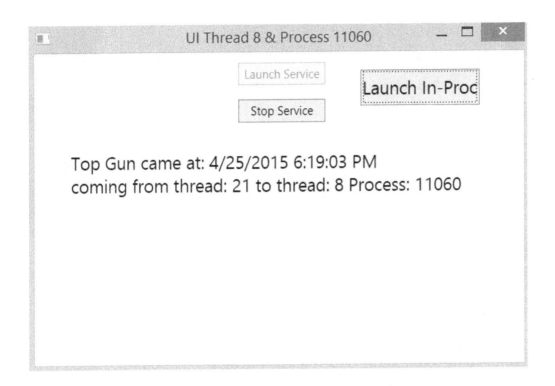

SERVICE INTEGRATION:-

In this section, I am going to do one integration test. Integration Test means End-to-End test. Therefore, here it will not have any mocked up data rather, it will go to database and do all the infrastructure calls and return the data. In order to do the same, I had a dependency on Entity Framework in my test project. Hence, first installed that, then I have created one test class Service Integration Test. Below is the snapshot of modified project.

Pragmatic WCF

▲ C# MovieLib.Tests
  ▷ 🔧 Properties
  ▷ ∎∎ References
    🗁 App.config
  ▷ C# MovieTests.cs
    🗁 packages.config
  ▷ 🗗 ServiceIntegrationTest.cs

In addition, after installing EF and referencing WCF assemblies; my references look like as shown below.

▲ ∎∎ References
  ∎∎ EntityFramework
  ∎∎ EntityFramework.SqlServer
  ∎∎ Microsoft.CSharp
  ∎∎ Microsoft.VisualStudio.QualityTools.UnitTestFramework
  ∎∎ Moq
  ∎∎ MovieLib.Contracts
  ∎∎ MovieLib.Core
  ∎∎ MovieLib.Data
  ∎∎ MovieLib.Services
  ∎∎ System
  ∎∎ System.ComponentModel.DataAnnotations
  ∎∎ System.Core
  ∎∎ System.Data
  ∎∎ System.Data.DataSetExtensions
  ∎∎ System.Runtime.Serialization
  ∎∎ System.ServiceModel
  ∎∎ System.Xml
  ∎∎ System.Xml.Linq

Then, in the test file I have used the below snippet. This is self-explanatory as all dependencies are explained in earlier section.

```
using System.Collections.Generic;
using System.ComponentModel;
using System.Linq;
using System.ServiceModel;
```

Pragmatic WCF

```
using System.ServiceModel.Channels;

using Microsoft.VisualStudio.TestTools.UnitTesting;

using MovieLib.Contracts;

using MovieLib.Services;


namespace MovieLib.Tests
{
    [TestClass]
    public class ServiceIntegrationTest
    {
        [TestMethod]
        public void Test_Movie_Name_Service()
        {
            string address = "net.pipe://localhost/MovieName";
            Binding binding = new NetNamedPipeBinding();


            ServiceHost host = new ServiceHost(typeof(MovieManager));


            host.AddServiceEndpoint(typeof (IMovieService), binding, address);


            host.Open();


            ChannelFactory<IMovieService> factory = new
ChannelFactory<IMovieService>(binding,new EndpointAddress(address));


            IMovieService proxy = factory.CreateChannel();


            IEnumerable<MovieData> data = proxy.GetDirectorNames();


            Assert.IsTrue(data.Count().Equals(11));
        }
    }
}
```

Now, when I run the test, then it will produce the below output.

Pragmatic WCF

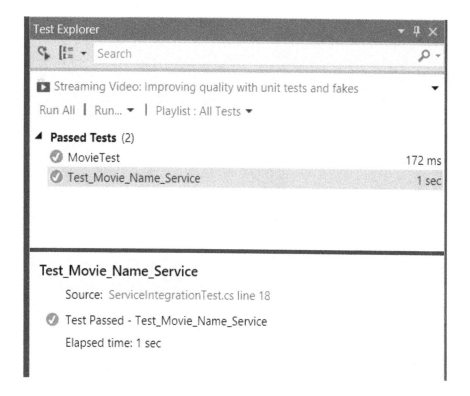

SUMMARY:-

In this section, we have covered variety of things like how to handle deadlock situation if we are trapped in the same. We also saw the situation, when deadlock situation arises. How to handle In-Process calls. How to delegate the service on the background thread. How to keep UI thread free for any kind of operations. In the end, we have covered one integration test.

Pragmatic WCF

WHAT DO you find in this CHAPTER?

- Introduction
- When to choose what
- Transport
- Binding configurations
- Send Timeout
- Max Received Message
- Sliding Timeout
- Behavior Configuration
- Throttling
- Summary

INTRODUCTION:-

In this section, we are going to discuss complete suite of different bindings available with WCF. Binding is one of the elements for building any WCF application. We have already seen basic usage of bindings in the previous sections. Now, let us go ahead and do little deep dive in Bindings. Bindings are nothing but transport mechanism for communication. They decide how the messages are going to be communicated. Different bindings have different meanings and usage. Now, let us discuss some of the bindings, which are most commonly used.

- HTTP Bindings (Basic and WS):- Travels on port 80 and can go through the firewall. By default, they are not secured but using certificates, these can be secured.

- TCP Bindings: - These are typically sit inside the Firewall. Since, these bindings sit inside the firewall, hence these are faster than HTTP bindings and secure as well.

- NetNamedPipeBinding: - These are fastest binding but limited to a single machine. So, this is used in a very specific scenario like In-Process Transaction, which I showed in the last section.

Pragmatic WCF

- UDP bindings: - In .Net 4.0 Microsoft introduced new binding that is similar to TCP but non-reliable. Nevertheless, this is limited to subnet.

- MSMQ Binding: - MSMQ has its own API. Therefore, in order to use the same we need to rely on its API. In addition, this is used for queuing and can work disconnected.

WHEN TO CHOOSE WHAT:-

In this section, we will see when to choose which binding. Below I have pasted one simple self-descriptive decision tree.

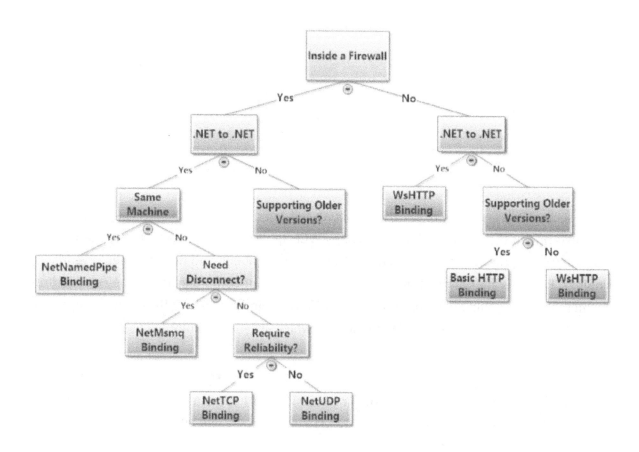

Let me explain the same. So, before choosing any binding first question we will ask is are we inside a firewall. Then if answer is no and we are using **.Net-To-.Net** communication then in that case, we can go for **WsHttpBinding** as it supports complete WS-* stack and many more

Pragmatic WCF

features than the basic one. Now, if Client is not **.Net-To-.Net**, then do you need to support older version of java clients or .Net 2.0 or below, then you can use **BasicHttpBinding**. Here, you will not get any out of the box features provided by WS-* stack but at least you can communicate.

However, if you are inside the firewall and client is not **.Net-to-.Net**, then you can ask Supporting Older Version question. Moreover, if it is a .Net client and inside the Firewall, then next question would be if it sits in the same machine or in other words it's local In Process only then you can use **NetNamedPipeBinding**. In addition, if the client is not on the same machine and it is more conventional like server on one machine and client on other, then next question I would ask is whether you need Disconnect. If the answer is yes, then you should use **NetMSMQBinding.** If the answer is no, then next question I would ask is whether you need reliability? Now, if you do not require reliability you can use **NetUDPBinding** otherwise **NetTcpBinding**. Therefore, this is the most common use case of before choosing any binding.

TRANSPORT:-

Transport level Sessions allow service to identify its clients. It keeps an open pipe means connection between service and client. In addition, handshaking between service and client makes it easy to identify who the client is. We will discuss this scenario in detail in coming chapters. Nevertheless, let me give a brief idea about the same. It appears in the callback scenario. In this case, service callback to the client. Moreover, for making the call service needs to know things about client like where the client is. Who the client is? Therefore, callbacks are only going to work when Transport Sessions are active. Now, there are few bindings, which support Transport level sessions out of the box.

- netTcpBinding: - Supports by default. No additional configuration needed.
- netNamedPipeBinding: - This also supports by default.
- wsHttpBinding: - This also supports but in conjunction with either reliability or security turned on.

So, whenever Transport sessions are needed; above listed characteristics are needed.

Pragmatic WCF

BINDING CONFIGURATIONS:-

In this section, we will discuss Binding Configurations. Binding Configurations is the place where in we can set the characteristics of Binding. Therefore, any binding configuration we set has to be set on both sides of the wire. No difference. Therefore, if you change the binding on the service side, you also need to change the same on the client side as well. So, now next question arises what do these Binding Configurations offer? They offer plethora of characteristics. Some of the most possible settings are listed below which we always use on day-to-day basis.

- Reliability
- Message Size
- Transaction Flow
- Ordered Messaging
- Inactivity Timeout
- Message Timeout

Any of these binding configurations can be set either declaratively or procedurally. Before writing any binding configuration, let us look at few attribute in detail.

- Reliability: - It provides End-to-End message transfer reliability. Therefore, turning reliability on means it will keep trying transferring message in case of network failures. This comes by default with TCP binding.

- Ordered Messaging: - Ordered messaging guarantees that messages which your sending has to be received in the same order the way it sent. Turning this feature on means each subsequent call will execute in the same order as it dispatched.

- In-Activity Timeout: - With reliability setting, there is one more setting come into picture called In-Activity Timeout. When you have a reliable session, you want to keep it open for a specific amount of time in which you are not receiving a message. It does support infinite value means you can keep it open indefinitely.

- As I said, Transport Sessions only available under certain conditions like use either TCP, IPC (namedPipe) or WsHTTP (with Reliability or Security turned on).

- Receive Timeout: - This setting is also similar to sliding value. Nevertheless, this is applicable for non-reliable sessions. It also supports infinite value.

Pragmatic WCF

- Send Timeout: - This attribute specifies the time that call will wait for a message to be processed. If it has not processed in a certain amount of time; it will get timeout and notifies that I have not received the response message yet.

- Message Size: - This is the maximum size of SOAP message. Default SOAP message size is 64K.

SEND TIMEOUT:-

The first setting, which I am going to discuss here, is Send Timeout Setting. This setting is one of the most useful settings during development. During production, I will leave the same as it is. The default timeout setting is 45 seconds; So, I think this is more than enough time for a service to respond. Services taking more than 45 seconds; then in that case developers need to revisit the service design and inspect the design what service is actually doing and fine-tune the same. Therefore, what I am going to do here is introduce a delay of 10 seconds in my service project as shown below in the snippet.

```
public IEnumerable<MovieData> GetDirectorNames()
    {
        Thread.Sleep(10000);
        List<MovieData> movieData = new List<MovieData>();

        try
        {
            IMovieRepository movieRepository = _iMovieRepository ?? new
MovieRepository();

            IEnumerable<Movie> movies = movieRepository.GetMovies();

            if (movies != null)
            {
                foreach (Movie movie in movies)
                {
                    // movieData.Add(movie.DirectorName);
```

Pragmatic WCF

```
                    movieData.Add(new MovieData()
                    {
                          DirectorName = movie.DirectorName
                    });
                }
            }
        }
        catch (Exception ex)
        {
            throw new ApplicationException("Something Messed Up : {0}",
ex.InnerException);
        }
        return movieData;
    }
}
}
```

After introducing delay, we need to configure the bindings at both the places means as shown below in the configs file.

```
<system.serviceModel>
    <services>
        <service name="MovieLib.Services.MovieManager">
            <endpoint address="net.tcp://localhost:8010/MovieService"
                    binding="netTcpBinding"
                    contract="MovieLib.Contracts.IMovieService"
                    bindingConfiguration="rahulTCP"/>

            <endpoint address="http://localhost/MovieService"
                    binding="basicHttpBinding"
                    contract="MovieLib.Contracts.IMovieService"/>
        </service>
        <service name="WindowsHostApplication.Services.MovieNameManager">
```

Pragmatic WCF

```xml
        <endpoint address="net.pipe://localhost/MovieName"
                  binding="netNamedPipeBinding"
                  contract="WindowsHostApplication.Contracts.IMovieName"/>
    </service>
  </services>
  <bindings>
    <netTcpBinding>
      <binding name="rahulTCP" sendTimeout="00:00:01">

      </binding>
    </netTcpBinding>
  </bindings>
  <client>
    <endpoint address="net.pipe://localhost/MovieName"
              binding="netNamedPipeBinding"
              contract="WindowsHostApplication.Contracts.IMovieName"/>
  </client>
  </system.serviceModel>
</configuration>
```

Similarly, in the client side as well.

```xml
<?xml version="1.0" encoding="utf-8" ?>
<configuration>
  <startup>
    <supportedRuntime version="v4.0" sku=".NETFramework,Version=v4.5" />
  </startup>
  <system.serviceModel>
    <client>
      <endpoint address="net.tcp://localhost:8010/MovieService"
                binding="netTcpBinding"
                contract="MovieLib.Contracts.IMovieService"
                name="1stEP"
                bindingConfiguration="rahulTCP"/>
```

Pragmatic WCF

```xml
        <endpoint address="http://localhost/MovieService"
                binding="basicHttpBinding"
                contract="MovieLib.Contracts.IMovieService"
                name="2ndEP"/>
        <endpoint address="net.tcp://localhost:8011/MovieName"
                binding="netTcpBinding"
                contract="MovieLib.Client.Contracts.IMovieName"/>
      </client>
    <bindings>
     <netTcpBinding>
       <binding name="rahulTCP" sendTimeout="00:00:01">
       </binding>
     </netTcpBinding>
    </bindings>
   </system.serviceModel>
</configuration>
```

One thing to note about this configuration; these configurations will not come into play until you attach them with the endpoint as if I have done above with the attribute **bindingConfiguration**. In addition, this timeout is of type timespan and here for showing exception I have purposely set it to 1 second.

▷ ● [System.TimeoutException]	("This request operation sent to net.tcp://localhost:8010/MovieService did not receive a reply within the configured timeout (00:00:01).
●ₐ _className	null
▷ ●ₐ _data	{System.Collections.ListDictionaryInternal}
●ₐ _dynamicMethods	null
●ₐ _exceptionMethod	null
●ₐ _exceptionMethodString	null
●ₐ _helpURL	null
● _HResult	-2146233083
▷ ●ₐ _innerException	null
▷ ●ₐ _ipForWatsonBuckets	195468372
● _message	🔍 ▾ "This request operation sent to net.tcp://localhost:8010/MovieService did not receive a reply within the configured timeout (00:00:01).
●ₐ _remoteStackIndex	1
●ₐ _remoteStackTraceString	🔍 ▾ "\r\nServer stack trace: \r\n at System.ServiceModel.Dispatcher.DuplexChannelBinder.Request(Message message, TimeSpan timeout)\
▷ ●ₐ _safeSerializationManager	{System.Runtime.Serialization.SafeSerializationManager}
●ₐ _source	null

Pragmatic WCF

MAX RECEIVED MESSAGE:-

Many a time it happens that Maximum size quota for incoming message exceeds **64K**, which is the default size. In order to handle this kind of situation; we can configure the same on both sides of the wire with Binding Configuration. Below is the configuration for handling the same.

```
<bindings>
  <netTcpBinding>
    <binding name="rahulTCP" sendTimeout="00:00:45" maxre|>
    </binding>
  </netTcpBinding>
</bindings>
</system.serviceModel>
</configuration>
```

```
    lockItem
    maxBufferPoolSize
    maxBufferSize
    maxConnections
    maxReceivedMessageSize
    openTimeout
    portSharingEnabled
    receiveTimeout
    transactionFlow
```

This property is of type **long**. Hence, I can set the value like shown below.

```
<bindings>

    <netTcpBinding>

        <binding name="rahulTCP" sendTimeout="00:00:45"
maxReceivedMessageSize="10000000">


        </binding>

    </netTcpBinding>

  </bindings>
```

Let us suppose you have two different values for the same setting on both sides of the wire. In that case, shorter one wins and its value will be considered as final value.

Pragmatic WCF

SLIDING TIMEOUT:-

Sliding Timeout works little differently. It is dependent on two core properties 1) Inactivity Timeout and 2) Receive Timeout. Therefore, the way it works is if you are using a non-reliable binding, only thing, which you need to worry, is receive timeout. However, if you are using reliable binding means TCP binding then you need to configure both the pieces explicitly. Below I am doing the same.

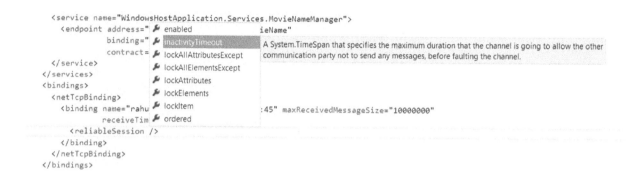

As you can see in the above snapshot, I also have option to enable reliable session. So, if I would have been using the same with **wsHttpBinding**; I would have done that. Nevertheless, since TCP is by default reliable hence this setting is not required. However, we do require **Inactivity Timeout** and **Receive Timeout** to be set here.

```
<bindings>
    <netTcpBinding>
        <binding name="rahulTCP" sendTimeout="00:00:45" maxReceivedMessageSize="10000000"
                receiveTimeout="00:00:05">
            <reliableSession inactivityTimeout="00:00:05"/>
        </binding>
    </netTcpBinding>
</bindings>
```

Same configuration I have done on the client side as well. Always remember this whatever, binding configuration you are doing, it needs to be done on both sides of the wire. However, all these settings are for open proxy. Hence, we need to broaden the scope of the proxy. It will not work with current code as we are opening the proxy on button click and closing the same in the

Pragmatic WCF

same event. With the above changes in place when I run the same and delay the button click by 5 seconds, then it gave me below error

Exception thrown by service.System.ServiceModel.CommunicationException: The socket connection was aborted. This could be caused by an error processing your message or a receive timeout being exceeded by the remote host, or an underlying network resource issue. Local socket timeout was '00:00:44.9200000'. ---> System.IO.IOException: The read operation failed, see inner exception. ---> System.ServiceModel.CommunicationException: The socket connection was aborted. This could be caused by an error processing your message or a receive timeout being exceeded by the remote host, or an underlying network resource issue. Local socket timeout was '00:00:44.9200000'.

It says socket connection Timeout because it exceeded the time allotted for sliding timeout. Default timeout for sliding case is 20 minutes. Nevertheless, you can keep infinite value as well. However, I do not recommend keeping proxy open for a long time, as I prefer stateless approach for the same. When I set the same to default value as shown below, my app started working fine as shown below.

```
<bindings>
    <netTcpBinding>
        <binding name="rahulTCP" sendTimeout="00:00:45" maxReceivedMessageSize="10000000"
                receiveTimeout="00:20:00">
          <reliableSession inactivityTimeout="00:10:00"/>
        </binding>
    </netTcpBinding>
</bindings>
```

Pragmatic WCF

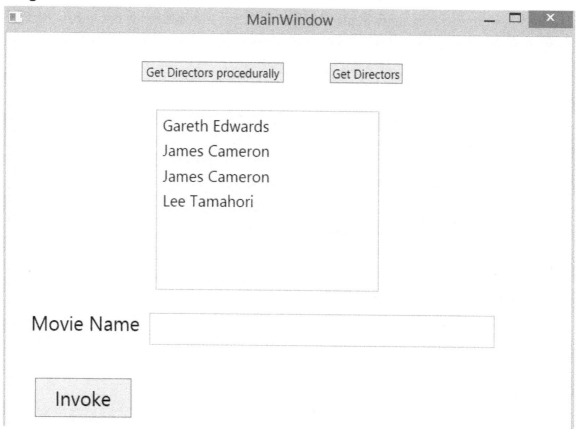

In addition, associated to reliable session I can also set ordering on both sides of the wire as shown below in the snippet.

```
<bindings>
    <netTcpBinding>
      <binding name="rahulTCP" sendTimeout="00:00:45" maxReceivedMessageSize="10000000"
              receiveTimeout="00:20:00">
        <reliableSession inactivityTimeout="00:10:00" ordered="true"/>
      </binding>
    </netTcpBinding>
  </bindings>
```

Pragmatic WCF

Behaviors are little different from binding configurations. These are characteristics of service. So, the behavior which I am going to discuss here is service behavior which means they are only known to service and only settable to service. Hence, client will have no idea of service behavior. Again like other settings service behaviors also can be set declaratively or inline. However, there is a catch here; with service behaviors, few settings, which can be set via code, only means inline. They cannot be administered via config file. Below, I have listed possible service behavior settings used often.

- Exception Details
- Metadata
- Throttling
- Concurrency
- Instancing

We will see each of them individually in coming chapter. However, let us see how to implement Service Behavior here. Below in the snippet, I have made one deliberate exception. Now, let us build the same and check the result without behavior first.

```csharp
public IEnumerable<MovieData> GetDirectorNames()
    {

        List<MovieData> movieData = new List<MovieData>();

        throw new Exception("Hello Unhandled Exception");
        IMovieRepository movieRepository = _iMovieRepository ?? new
MovieRepository();

        IEnumerable<Movie> movies = movieRepository.GetMovies();

        if (movies != null)
        {
            foreach (Movie movie in movies)
            {
                movieData.Add(new MovieData()
                {
```

Pragmatic WCF

```
                    DirectorName = movie.DirectorName
            });
        }
    }



        return movieData;

    }
```

```
namespace MovieLib.Proxies
{
    6 references
    public class MovieClient : ClientBase<IMovieService>, IMovieService
    {
        1 reference
        public MovieClient(string endpointName):base(endpointName)
        {

        }

        1 reference
        public MovieClient(Binding binding, End
        {

        }
        7 references | ● 0/2 passing
        public IEnumerable<MovieData> GetDirec
        {

            return Channel.GetDirectorNames();
        }
    }
}
```

> ⚠ **FaultException was unhandled**   ✕
>
> An unhandled exception of type
> 'System.ServiceModel.FaultException' occurred in
> mscorlib.dll
>
> Additional information: The server was unable to process the
> request due to an internal error. For more information about
>
> **Troubleshooting tips:**
>
> Get general help for this exception.
>
> Search for more Help Online...
>
> **Exception settings:**
> ☐ Break when this exception type is thrown
>
> **Actions:**
> View Detail...
> Copy exception detail to the clipboard
> Open exception settings

As you can see in the above screenshot, it is telling that turn on the service behavior to see the exact error message. Now, let me go ahead and enable the same in the app.config file. Remember, since this is service behavior, hence it needs to enable on the service side only.

Pragmatic WCF

```
    <bindings>
      <netTcpBinding>
        <binding name="rahulTCP" sendTimeout="00:00:45" maxReceivedMessageSize="10000000"
                 receiveTimeout="00:20:00">
                            ─inactivityTimeout="00:10:00" ordered="true"/>
         ┌─────────────────────────────┐
         │ <!-- !--                     │
         │ <? ?                         │
      </b│ 🔲 endpointBehaviors         │
      <be│ 🔲 serviceBehaviors          │
         └─────────────────────────────┘
         <│
    </behaviors>
```

As you can see in the options, there are two behaviors. Endpoint behavior we will see in coming chapter. Now, let me go ahead and add service behavior.

```
<system.serviceModel>
    <services>
        <service name="MovieLib.Services.MovieManager" behaviorConfiguration="rahulTCP">
            <endpoint address="net.tcp://localhost:8010/MovieService"
                    binding="netTcpBinding"
                    contract="MovieLib.Contracts.IMovieService"
                    bindingConfiguration="rahulTCP"/>


            <endpoint address="http://localhost/MovieService"
                    binding="basicHttpBinding"
                    contract="MovieLib.Contracts.IMovieService"/>

        </service>
        <service name="WindowsHostApplication.Services.MovieNameManager">
            <endpoint address="net.pipe://localhost/MovieName"
                    binding="netNamedPipeBinding"
                    contract="WindowsHostApplication.Contracts.IMovieName"/>

        </service>
    </services>
    <bindings>
        <netTcpBinding>
            <binding name="rahulTCP" sendTimeout="00:00:45" maxReceivedMessageSize="10000000"
                    receiveTimeout="00:20:00">
                <reliableSession inactivityTimeout="00:10:00" ordered="true"/>
```

Pragmatic WCF

```
        </binding>
      </netTcpBinding>
    </bindings>
    <behaviors>
      <serviceBehaviors>
        <behavior name="rahulTCP">
          <serviceDebug includeExceptionDetailInFaults="true"/>
        </behavior>
      </serviceBehaviors>
    </behaviors>
    <client>
      <endpoint address="net.pipe://localhost/MovieName"
                binding="netNamedPipeBinding"
                contract="WindowsHostApplication.Contracts.IMovieName"/>
    </client>
  </system.serviceModel>
```

Let me explain the config section first. Here, I have added Service behavior section then I gave it a name and lastly I included Service Debug attribute to show the exception details. Then, I have assigned my service with this behavior. One more point to note here, above example is called named behavior as I have given name to behavior. I can also write service behavior without any name and then in that case it will point to that service by default. With the above changes in place, when I run the app, then it will again throw the exception, but this time it gave me additional information.

Pragmatic WCF

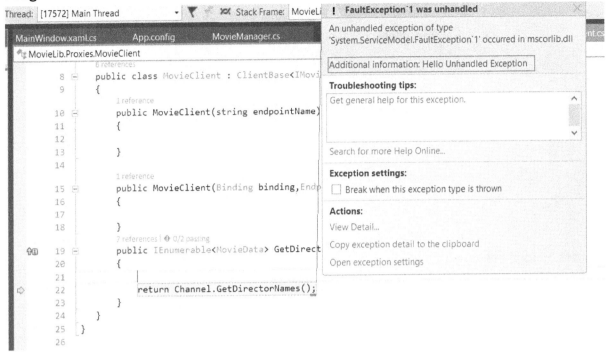

Now, let us go ahead and achieve the same thing programmatically. Before, that let me just comment out the config changes which I just done.

```
private void Btnlaunch_Click(object sender, RoutedEventArgs e)
    {
        _serviceHost = new ServiceHost(typeof(MovieManager));
        _serviceHostMovieName = new ServiceHost(typeof(MovieNameManager));


        ServiceDebugBehavior behavior =
_serviceHost.Description.Behaviors.Find<ServiceDebugBehavior>();


        if (behavior == null)
        {
            behavior = new ServiceDebugBehavior();
            behavior.IncludeExceptionDetailInFaults = true;
            _serviceHost.Description.Behaviors.Add(behavior);
        }
        else
```

Pragmatic WCF

```
        {
                behavior.IncludeExceptionDetailInFaults = true;
        }


        _serviceHost.Open();
        _serviceHostMovieName.Open();
        Btnlaunch.IsEnabled = false;
        BtnStop.IsEnabled = true;


    }
```

So here before opening the host, I have added the service behavior programmatically and checked for null check as well. Now, one more point to note here is that WCF by default adds little behavior to the service and service debug is one of them but by default, it is set to false. So, if behavior is not null then just set the property to true. With the above changes in place, when I ran the same it gave me the same error.

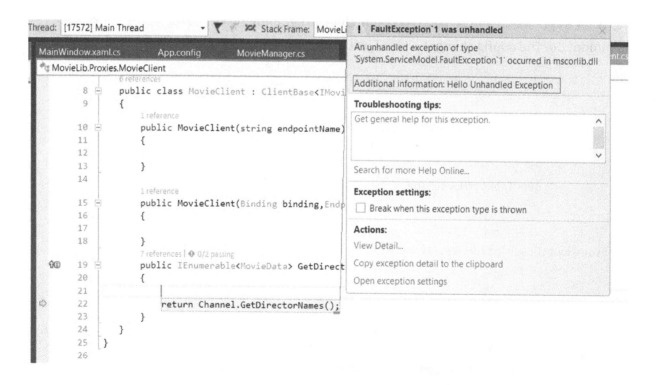

Now, let us see how to set the same inline. Before doing the same just remove the earlier code and put the below one-liner before movie manager class.

Pragmatic WCF

```csharp
[ServiceBehavior(IncludeExceptionDetailInFaults = true)]
    public class MovieManager : IMovieService
```

With the above change as well. I will see the same message what we saw earlier.

THROTTLING:-

There are some other settings as well which you can set in service behavior and throttling is one of them. Let us see the same in action.

Therefore, above attributes you can go ahead and set. Nevertheless, we use below shown properties.

```xml
<behaviors>
    <serviceBehaviors>
      <behavior>
        <serviceDebug includeExceptionDetailInFaults="true"/>
        <serviceThrottling maxConcurrentSessions="100"
                           maxConcurrentCalls="16"
                           maxConcurrentInstances="116"/>
      </behavior>
    </serviceBehaviors>
  </behaviors>
```

Pragmatic WCF

Now, let me explain the same. We will see the same in detail in coming chapter. However, briefly I can tell you that max concurrent sessions is the total no of open transport sessions that can exist at one point of time. Concurrent calls is the no of calls that can be processed at the same time by service. Concurrent instance depends on the instance mode; hence, we will see this in detail in Instancing chapter.

SUMMARY:-

In this chapter, we have covered variety of topics covering behavior and binding configuration. We have started with binding configuration wherein we saw how to setup bindings both sides of the wire. While setting Binding configuration, we also saw variety of properties like sliding timeout, send timeout, max-received message and many others. Then, in the behavior configuration; we have seen how to set the same procedurally, programmatically and declaratively.

Pragmatic WCF

WHAT DO you find in this CHAPTER?

- Introduction
- What is Metadata
- Metadata Exposure
- Adding Behavior
- Adding Service Reference
- Adding Client Code
- Adding Mex Endpoint
- Adding Mex Programmatically
- Summary

INTRODUCTION:-

In this section, we will cover Metadata exchange topic. One of the biggest difference between WCF and its cousin technology Web API is its ability to expose metadata. When you are dealing with Web API, you have to have well documented service model API, so that client knows how to access it. With WCF, you have the idea of Metadata Exchange.

WHAT IS METADATA:-

Metadata is shape and characteristics of service; it is pretty much everything about service means what contracts it implements, what data contract it uses both request and response, all the characteristics of binding etc. All these bits are part of metadata and this is exposed in the form of **WSDL**. Now, metadata is exposed in a different way through special address and potential consumers do have this special address to obtain information. In order to gain access to the service client do not need to know anything about service as with visual studio they can use **ASR** (Add Service Reference). When, you add this service reference; you point to specific address and Visual Studio automatically generates for you. So, Data-Contracts, Service-Contracts, client proxies will get auto generated. One more point to note here, it is not Visual Studio is generating all these code for you. However, visual studio is using one utility behind the scene that **svcutil.exe**.

Pragmatic WCF

The exposure of metadata is done with Service behavior. In the last chapter, we have seen how to use Service Behavior. Behavior can be exposed in two forms. First way is using HTTP through a base address. It requires **<serviceMetadata>** behavior with **httpGetEnabled** property set to true. The other way of doing this by using MEX endpoint on TCP, IPC (namedPipe) or HTTP. This also requires **<serviceMetadata>** behavior but it does not require **httpGetEnabled** property. Now, this can also be achieved programmatically. Now, let us go ahead and see the same in action.

ADDING BEHAVIOR:-

Here in this section I have added behavior in the app.config of Windows Host.

```xml
<behaviors>
    <serviceBehaviors>
      <behavior>
        <serviceMetadata httpGetEnabled="true"/>
      </behavior>
    </serviceBehaviors>
  </behaviors>
```

I have also added base address for the same as shown below.

```xml
<system.serviceModel>
   <services>
     <service name="MovieLib.Services.MovieManager">
       <host>
         <baseAddresses>
           <add baseAddress="http://localhost:8012"/>
         </baseAddresses>
       </host>

       <endpoint address="net.tcp://localhost:8010/MovieService"
```

Pragmatic WCF

```
            binding="netTcpBinding"
            contract="MovieLib.Contracts.IMovieService" />
    <endpoint address="http://localhost/MovieService"
            binding="basicHttpBinding"
            contract="MovieLib.Contracts.IMovieService"/>
  </service>
 </services>
 <behaviors>
   <serviceBehaviors>
     <behavior>
       <serviceMetadata httpGetEnabled="true"/>
     </behavior>
   </serviceBehaviors>
 </behaviors>
</system.serviceModel>
```

In the first setting I have added the service Metadata with httpGetEnabled set to true then, I have added the host section and in that, I have added the base address. Now, let us go ahead and add Service Reference.

ADDING SERVICE REFERENCE:-

In order to add Service Reference in the client code as shown, I need to run the Console Host out of visual studio. And the best way to run the Console Host out of visual studio is via exe in bin folder of the Console Host project. Run this Exe as Admin.

```
C:\Rahul\My Experiments\MovieLibWCF\MovieLib\ConsoleHostApplication\bi...
Service Launched,Press Enter to Exit!
```

Pragmatic WCF

Then, go to client project and then right-click on the reference and add Service Reference and then paste the base address and click on Go button. It will list the all the methods we are using with this service. In this case one method, which is **GetDirectorNames**.

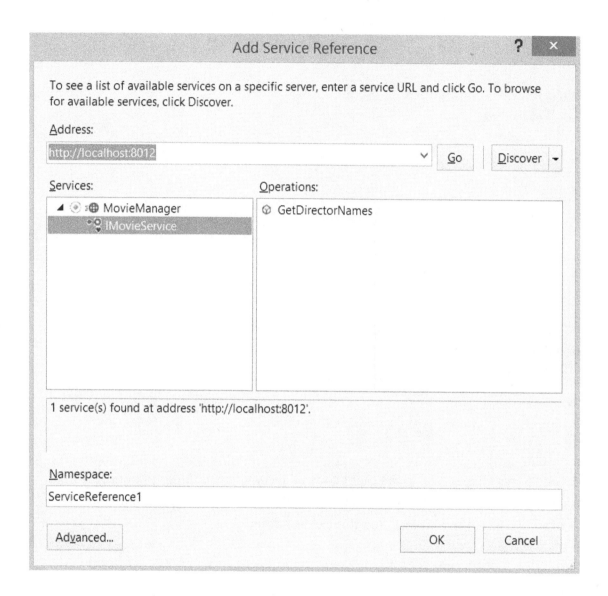

Namespace, which you are seeing in the above screen shot, is nothing but CLR namespace. Now, just go ahead and say ok. Then, it will add the all required stuffs in client project as shown below in the screen shot.

Pragmatic WCF

In order to see the stuffs it generated for me on the client side; click on show all files and it will list all.

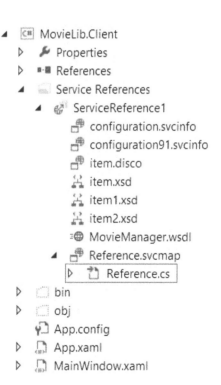

References.cs is the auto-generated code. Therefore, if you see the file it contains everything but it looks quite clumsy.

Pragmatic WCF

```
//----------------------------------------------------------------------------
// <auto-generated>
//     This code was generated by a tool.
//     Runtime Version:4.0.30319.34014
//
//     Changes to this file may cause incorrect behavior and will be lost if
//     the code is regenerated.
// </auto-generated>
//----------------------------------------------------------------------------

namespace MovieLib.Client.ServiceReference1 {


    [System.CodeDom.Compiler.GeneratedCodeAttribute("System.ServiceModel", "4.0.0.0")]

[System.ServiceModel.ServiceContractAttribute(ConfigurationName="ServiceReference1.IMovie
Service")]
    public interface IMovieService {


[System.ServiceModel.OperationContractAttribute(Action="http://tempuri.org/IMovieService/
GetDirectorNames",
ReplyAction="http://tempuri.org/IMovieService/GetDirectorNamesResponse")]
        MovieLib.Contracts.MovieData[] GetDirectorNames();


[System.ServiceModel.OperationContractAttribute(Action="http://tempuri.org/IMovieService/
GetDirectorNames",
ReplyAction="http://tempuri.org/IMovieService/GetDirectorNamesResponse")]
        System.Threading.Tasks.Task<MovieLib.Contracts.MovieData[]>
GetDirectorNamesAsync();
    }


    [System.CodeDom.Compiler.GeneratedCodeAttribute("System.ServiceModel", "4.0.0.0")]
    public interface IMovieServiceChannel :
MovieLib.Client.ServiceReference1.IMovieService, System.ServiceModel.IClientChannel {
    }
```

Pragmatic WCF

```csharp
[System.Diagnostics.DebuggerStepThroughAttribute()]
[System.CodeDom.Compiler.GeneratedCodeAttribute("System.ServiceModel", "4.0.0.0")]
public partial class MovieServiceClient :
System.ServiceModel.ClientBase<MovieLib.Client.ServiceReference1.IMovieService>,
MovieLib.Client.ServiceReference1.IMovieService {


    public MovieServiceClient() {
    }


    public MovieServiceClient(string endpointConfigurationName) :
            base(endpointConfigurationName) {
    }


    public MovieServiceClient(string endpointConfigurationName, string remoteAddress)
:
            base(endpointConfigurationName, remoteAddress) {
    }


    public MovieServiceClient(string endpointConfigurationName,
System.ServiceModel.EndpointAddress remoteAddress) :
            base(endpointConfigurationName, remoteAddress) {
    }


    public MovieServiceClient(System.ServiceModel.Channels.Binding binding,
System.ServiceModel.EndpointAddress remoteAddress) :
            base(binding, remoteAddress) {
    }


    public MovieLib.Contracts.MovieData[] GetDirectorNames() {
        return base.Channel.GetDirectorNames();
    }


    public System.Threading.Tasks.Task<MovieLib.Contracts.MovieData[]>
GetDirectorNamesAsync() {
        return base.Channel.GetDirectorNamesAsync();
    }
```

Pragmatic WCF

```
        }
}
```

It also modified my App.config file.

```xml
<?xml version="1.0" encoding="utf-8" ?>
<configuration>
  <startup>
    <supportedRuntime version="v4.0" sku=".NETFramework,Version=v4.5" />
  </startup>
  <system.serviceModel>
    <bindings>
      <basicHttpBinding>
        <binding name="BasicHttpBinding_IMovieService" />
      </basicHttpBinding>
      <netTcpBinding>
        <binding name="NetTcpBinding_IMovieService" />
      </netTcpBinding>
    </bindings>
    <client>
      <endpoint address="net.tcp://localhost:8010/MovieService" binding="netTcpBinding"
        contract="MovieLib.Contracts.IMovieService" name="1stEP" />
      <endpoint address="http://localhost/MovieService" binding="basicHttpBinding"
        contract="MovieLib.Contracts.IMovieService" name="2ndEP" />
      <endpoint address="net.tcp://localhost:8011/MovieName" binding="netTcpBinding"
        contract="MovieLib.Client.Contracts.IMovieName" />


      <endpoint address="net.tcp://localhost:8010/MovieService" binding="netTcpBinding"
        bindingConfiguration="NetTcpBinding_IMovieService"
contract="ServiceReference1.IMovieService"
        name="NetTcpBinding_IMovieService">
        <identity>
          <userPrincipalName value="Rahul_Sahay@amer.dell.com" />
        </identity>
```

Pragmatic WCF

```
        </endpoint>
        <!--<endpoint address="http://localhost/MovieService" binding="basicHttpBinding"
            bindingConfiguration="BasicHttpBinding_IMovieService"
contract="ServiceReference1.IMovieService"
            name="BasicHttpBinding_IMovieService" />-->
    </client>
    </system.serviceModel>
</configuration>
```

ADDING CLIENT CODE:-

Now, let us go ahead and add client code as shown below.

```csharp
private void Button_Click_2(object sender, RoutedEventArgs e)
    {
        MovieServiceClient proxy = new MovieServiceClient();

        IEnumerable<MovieData> datas = proxy.GetDirectorNames();

        if (datas != null)
        {
            LstDirectors.ItemsSource = datas;
        }

        proxy.Close();

    }
```

This code is also simple. Here, I have used the code, which is generated by Visual Studio, which means I have used the service reference to create the proxy 1st, and then I made the call to fetch the Directors and list the same. I have also introduced one new button fetch the button via service reference.

Pragmatic WCF

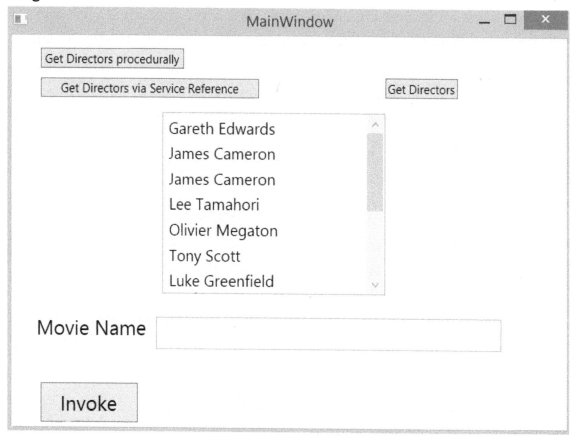

ADDING MEX ENDPOINT:-

To add a Mex Endpoint, I can simply go ahead and the same with one new endpoint as shown below in the config file.

```
<system.serviceModel>
    <services>
      <service name="MovieLib.Services.MovieManager">
        <host>
          <baseAddresses>
            <add baseAddress="http://localhost:8012"/>
            <add baseAddress="net.tcp://localhost:8010/MovieService"/>
          </baseAddresses>
        </host>

        <endpoint address=""
                  binding="netTcpBinding"
```

Pragmatic WCF

```
            contract="MovieLib.Contracts.IMovieService" />
    <endpoint address="http://localhost/MovieService"
            binding="basicHttpBinding"
            contract="MovieLib.Contracts.IMovieService"/>
  <endpoint address="MEX"
            binding="mexTcpBinding"
            contract="IMetadataExchange"/>
  </service>
 </services>
 <behaviors>
  <serviceBehaviors>
   <behavior>
     <serviceMetadata httpGetEnabled="true"/>
   </behavior>
  </serviceBehaviors>
 </behaviors>
</system.serviceModel>
```

Let me explain the code a bit. Therefore, as you can see I have added another base address for TCP binding and from TCP endpoint, I have removed the address, as it is not required. In addition, here I have added one additional endpoint for MEX with **mexTcpBinding** and **IMetadataExchange**. Now, in order to add another service reference again I need to build the app and launch the host outside visual studio. Then, in the client project when I add the service reference with the following address "**net.tcp://localhost:8010/MovieService/mex**", it will produce me the below output.

Pragmatic WCF

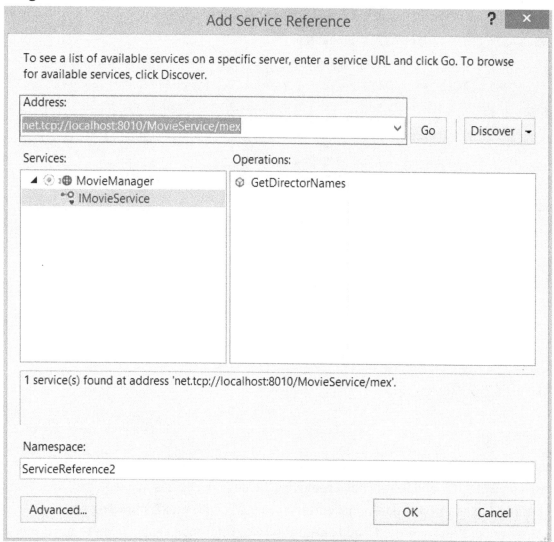

In this section, we will achieve the same thing but programmatically. So before doing that I just need to comment out the new Mex endpoint, which I added in the config file. I have also commented host and behavior section. Now, below is the simple snippet for adding Mex programmatically.

```
using System;
using System.ServiceModel;
using System.ServiceModel.Channels;
```

Pragmatic WCF

```csharp
using System.ServiceModel.Description;

using MovieLib.Contracts;

using MovieLib.Services;


namespace ConsoleHostApplication

{

    class Program

    {

        static void Main(string[] args)

        {

            ServiceHost hostMovieManager = new ServiceHost(typeof(MovieManager),new
Uri("http://localhost:8012"),

                new Uri("net.tcp://localhost:8010/MovieService"));


            ServiceMetadataBehavior behavior =
hostMovieManager.Description.Behaviors.Find<ServiceMetadataBehavior>();


            if (behavior == null)

            {

                behavior = new ServiceMetadataBehavior();

                behavior.HttpGetEnabled = true;

                hostMovieManager.Description.Behaviors.Add(behavior);

            }

            hostMovieManager.Open();

            Console.WriteLine("Service Launched,Press Enter to Exit!");

            Console.ReadLine();

            hostMovieManager.Close();

        }

    }

}
```

Now, let me explain code here. As you can see, first I have added the base addresses as I have
done in the config file. As you can see, second argument is a param argument. Then, I went
ahead and find the metadata. Then, I have null checked for behavior and then added the
required properties. One point to note that WCF will not add Metadata behavior by default

Pragmatic WCF

hence no need for else condition here. With this change in place when I go ahead build the same and try to locate the service reference, then it should produce me the below results.

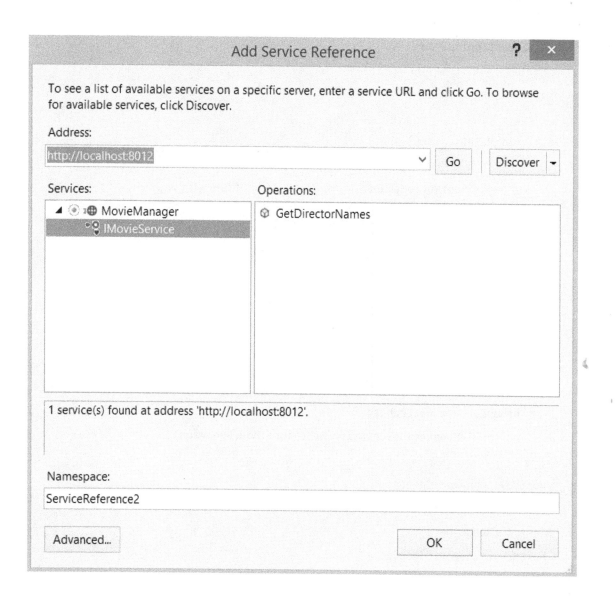

SUMMARY:-

In this chapter, we have covered MEX endpoints. We have also seen how to use it to add service reference to our client code based on the base addresses. We have seen for both TCP and HTTP protocols. We have also seen how to add the same procedurally and

Pragmatic WCF

programmatically. We also had a quick look on the auto-generated code by Visual Studio. In the next section, we will delve further and see how Instancing and concurrency works.

Pragmatic WCF

CHAPTER 8: INSTANCING & CONCURRENCY

WHAT DO you find in this CHAPTER?

- Introduction
- Per Call
- Per Session
- Single Session
- Per Call Demo
- Per Session Demo
- Singleton Demo
- Session Mode
- Binding Enforcement
- Concurrency
- Single Concurrency
- Multiple Concurrency
- Re-Entrant Concurrency
- Client Code Setup
- Per Call Test
- Per Session Test
- Singleton Test
- Per Call Multiple Test
- Per Session Multiple Test
- Singleton Multiple Test
- Task Test
- Summary

Pragmatic WCF

INTRODUCTION:-

In this section, I am going to cover two major topics and that is instancing and concurrency. In the first segment of this chapter, we will cover instancing and then we cover concurrency. Instancing literally means the instance of service. Here instancing is meant to process a call to handle the incoming call. In this case, we will see different modes of instancing and associated scenarios when these kind of instancing modes are required. Therefore, this is good as it eludes the concept of maintaining state something, which you cannot do in WEB API but obviously achieve in WCF. Therefore, this is one of biggest difference between WEB API and WCF as Web API is always stateless does not get any State assistance however, WCF can be HTTP but still manages state at the host side. There are three modes of instantiation. They are-

- Per Call
- Per Session (Default)
- Single

PER CALL:-

Per Call is pretty much based on its name. It means any call to a service will be serviced by a brand new instance of service. It means whenever client makes a call; host will new up the service, perform the operation and then do the housekeeping means disposes the instance, if it implements **IDisposable** pattern on it. This is the case even when client keeps proxy open. Now, this is the most scalable solution, nothing will be left in memory, and it is my preferred method unless I need state. Therefore, it is very clear with Per Call that I cannot hold state; so even if I have class-scoped variable then during the other call it will be lost, as service will new up the instance. For maintaining state, I need to use Per Session option, which we will discuss in a moment.

PER SESSION:-

Per Session, instancing is different. In this case, host will new up the instance on the first call from proxy. Therefore, while that proxy is open all calls from that proxy will be served by the same service instance. This means you can hold states. You can have class-scoped variables, which can be changed in one call, and the next call can actually see that change. Nevertheless, you must consider locking before updating state. We will see these scenarios when we get into concurrency. Moreover, when proxy is closed, infrastructure makes one final call to dispose the

Pragmatic WCF

service instance. Therefore, lifetime of a service is directly proportional to lifetime of proxy. This is why Per Session is default in WCF as this follows the exact same path of conventional object behavior. Now, there are few points to note here. When we use Per Session Instancing, we must have **Transport Session enabled**. Therefore, to have Transport Session present we must follow either of below rules:-

- TCP Binding
- Named Pipe Binding
- WsHttpBinding with Reliability or Security turned on.

One more important point to note here, let us suppose that you are not following any of the above rules then in that case Per Session mode will gracefully downgrade to Per Call mode.

SINGLE SESSION:-

Last but not the least is Single Session instancing. Also known as Singleton instance. As the nomenclature suggests this is based on the Singleton Pattern. It means host news up the service when opened. This also means there will be one and only one service instance serving up different calls from different clients. This can also hold in-memory state, which means you, can refer the old values what you have set on class-scoped variables during the last visit. Nevertheless, you must consider locking before doing any updates as the scope of this instance is wide level as it is shared between the clients. In Per Session we used to share but with the same client or same proxy. Service is not going to dispose the instance until host is closed. So, lifetime of instance is not equated to client but with the lifetime of host.

PER CALL DEMO:-

In order to set the service behavior to per call we will use **InstanceContextMode** as shown below in the screen shot. Moreover, from the enum value will select **PerCall**.

Pragmatic WCF

```
[ServiceBehavior(InstanceContextMode = InstanceContextMode)]
6 references
public class MovieManager : IMovieSe
{
    private IMovieRepository _iMovie
    0 references
    public MovieManager()
    {

    }
}
```

	InstanceContextMode
	InstanceContextMode.PerCall
	InstanceContextMode.PerSession
	InstanceContextMode.Single
	new InstanceContextMode()

With this when I build the app and run the same, and then you will not observe any difference. Nevertheless, then I will add some additional code to show what is meant by Per Call.

Pragmatic WCF

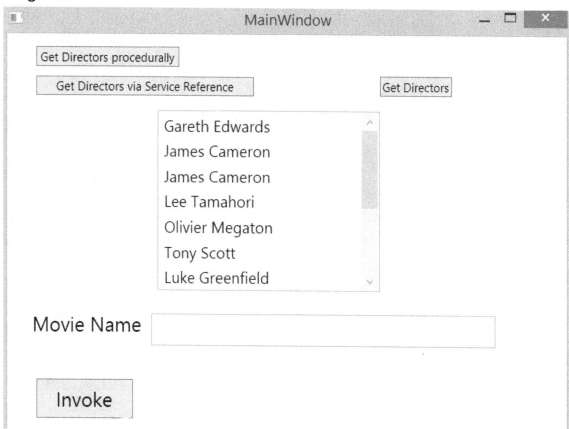

Now, let us go ahead do the changes. I am going to add one class scoped variable just to set the counter.

```
using System;
using System.Collections;
using System.Collections.Generic;
using System.Linq;
using System.ServiceModel;
using System.Threading;
using MovieLib.Contracts;
using MovieLib.Data.Entities;
using MovieLib.Data.Repositories;
using MovieLib.Data.Repository_Interfaces;
```

Pragmatic WCF

```csharp
namespace MovieLib.Services
{
    [ServiceBehavior(InstanceContextMode = InstanceContextMode.PerCall)]
    public class MovieManager : IMovieService
    {
        private IMovieRepository _iMovieRepository;
        private int _counter = 0;
        public MovieManager()
        {

        }


        public MovieManager(IMovieRepository iMovieRepository)
        {
            _iMovieRepository = iMovieRepository;
        }
        public IEnumerable<MovieData> GetDirectorNames()
        {

            List<MovieData> movieData = new List<MovieData>();


            try
            {
                IMovieRepository movieRepository = _iMovieRepository ?? new
MovieRepository();

                IEnumerable<Movie> movies = movieRepository.GetMovies();

                if (movies != null)
                {
                    foreach (Movie movie in movies)
                    {
                        movieData.Add(new MovieData()
                        {
                            DirectorName = movie.DirectorName
                        });
```

Pragmatic WCF

```
                }
            }
            _counter++;
            Console.WriteLine("Counter:- {0}",_counter);
        }

        catch (Exception ex)
        {
            string.Format("Something messed up - {0}", ex.Message);
        }
        return movieData;
    }
  }
}
```

Now, let me explain the code a bit. This counter variable every time is getting incremented in Get Directors call. Moreover, this incremented value is being printed on the same console host. Nevertheless, this will always-print 1 as per call literally means per call; it will not persist any value. Also, let me go ahead and introduce class-scoped variable on the client side.

```
using System;
using System.Collections.Generic;
using System.ServiceModel;
using System.ServiceModel.Channels;
using System.Windows;
using MovieLib.Client.Contracts;
using MovieLib.Client.ServiceReference1;
using MovieLib.Contracts;
using MovieLib.Proxies;

namespace MovieLib.Client
{
    /// <summary>
```

Pragmatic WCF

```csharp
    /// Interaction logic for MainWindow.xaml
    /// </summary>

public partial class MainWindow : Window
{
    private MovieClient proxyClient = null;
    public MainWindow()
    {
        InitializeComponent();
        proxyClient = new MovieClient("1stEP");
    }


    private void Button_Click(object sender, RoutedEventArgs e)
    {
        // MovieClient proxyClient = new MovieClient("1stEP");

        try
        {
            IEnumerable<MovieData> data = proxyClient.GetDirectorNames();

            if (data != null)
            {
                LstDirectors.ItemsSource = data;

            }


            //   proxyClient.Close();
        }
        catch (Exception ex)
        {
            MessageBox.Show("Exception thrown by service." + ex);
        }
    }


    private void Button_Click_1(object sender, RoutedEventArgs e)
```

Pragmatic WCF

```
        {
                EndpointAddress address = new
EndpointAddress("net.tcp://localhost:8010/MovieService");
                Binding binding = new NetTcpBinding();


                MovieClient proxyClient = new MovieClient(binding, address);


                IEnumerable<MovieData> data = proxyClient.GetDirectorNames();


                if (data != null)
                {
                    LstDirectors.ItemsSource = data;
                }


                proxyClient.Close();
        }


        private void btnInvoke_Click(object sender, RoutedEventArgs e)
        {
                EndpointAddress address = new
EndpointAddress("net.tcp://localhost:8011/MovieName");
                Binding binding = new NetTcpBinding();


                ChannelFactory<IMovieName> factory = new ChannelFactory<IMovieName>(binding,
address);


                //ChannelFactory<IMovieName> factory = new ChannelFactory<IMovieName>("");


                IMovieName proxy = factory.CreateChannel();


                string value = txtMovieName.Text;
                proxy.ShowMovie(value);


                factory.Close();
        }


        private void Button_Click_2(object sender, RoutedEventArgs e)
```

Pragmatic WCF

```
        {
            MovieServiceClient proxy = new MovieServiceClient();

            IEnumerable<MovieData> datas = proxy.GetDirectorNames();

            if (datas != null)
            {
                LstDirectors.ItemsSource = datas;
            }

            proxy.Close();


        }


    }
}
```

In the above client code for the event of **Button_Click** I have introduced class wide variable. Now, let us build and test the app. Therefore, below I invoked the same call 5 times and every time I got the counter as one.

Pragmatic WCF

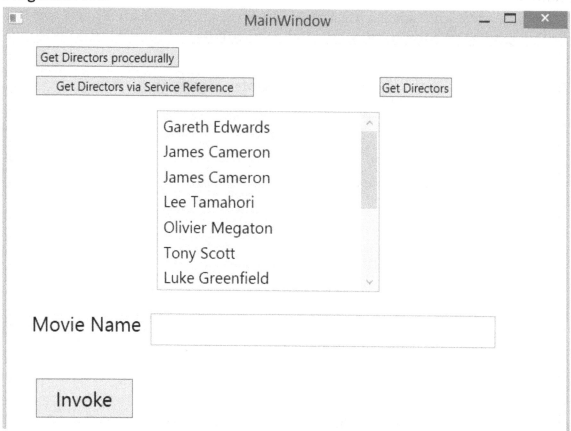

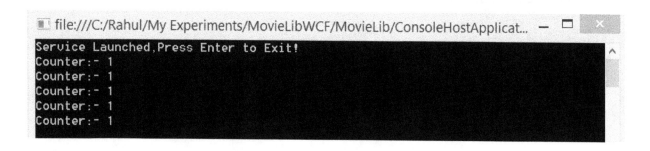

PER SESSION DEMO:-

In this section, I will do one change and off-course that is obvious; changing the behavior to **PerSession**. Below is the change for the same.

```
[ServiceBehavior(InstanceContextMode = InstanceContextMode.PerSession)]
```

Pragmatic WCF

Moreover, other things will remain same. Now, let us build the app and test the same.
Therefore, now it produced me the stateful result.

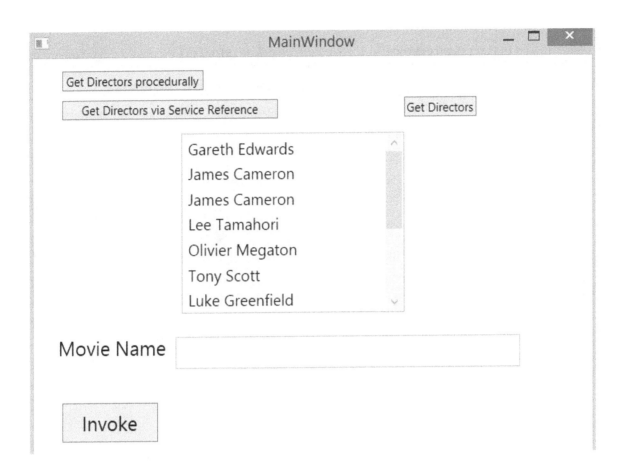

Pragmatic WCF

SINGLETON DEMO:-

In this section, I will pull two versions of client; one directly from Visual Studio and another one from bin directory of client project. However, before that let me set the behavior to single as shown below in the snippet.

```
[ServiceBehavior(InstanceContextMode = InstanceContextMode.Single)]
```

Now let us run the app. As soon as I clicked on Get Directors, it printed counter one.

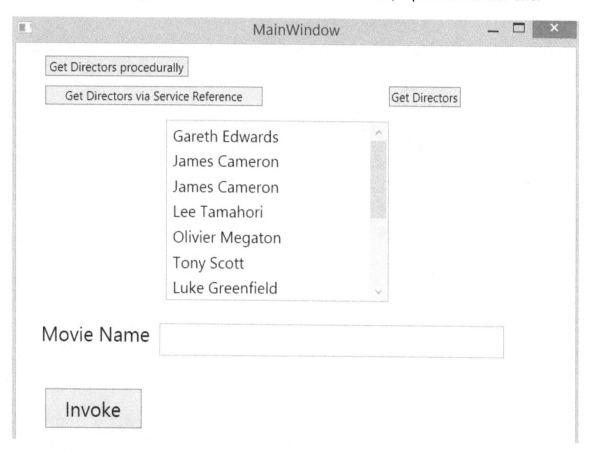

Then, I invoked different client from bin directory and then again clicked Get Directors. It produced me the below output.

Pragmatic WCF

```
file:///C:/Rahul/My Experiments/MovieLibWCF/MovieLib/ConsoleHostApplicat...
Service Launched,Press Enter to Exit!
Counter:- 1
Counter:- 2
```

Which means all different clients will share the same singleton instance of service. However, if you change the behavior to per session and repeat the similar operation running one client from VS and running other independently, then you will get result similar to shown below.

```
file:///C:/Rahul/My Experiments/MovieLibWCF/MovieLib/ConsoleHostApplicat...
Service Launched,Press Enter to Exit!
Counter:- 1
Counter:- 1
Counter:- 2
Counter:- 2
```

Here, it means each individual client maintains its own session.

SESSION MODE:-

Session Mode property configures the requirement mode for the Transport Session. Therefore, as I said earlier Transport Session will be available to you if you use TCP, IPC or WS HTTP Binding with Reliability or Security turned on. Now, there are three modes of Session Modes. They are-

- Allowed (Default):- In this case, I can set session mode to "**allowed**" and set binding to Basic HTTP Binding. Then in that case, I will not be having Transport Session available. Therefore, in that case Per Session service will behave like Per Call. There are other settings associated to this, which we will look in the demo.

- Required: - Required means it will require Transport Session binding setup.

Pragmatic WCF

- Not Allowed: - In this case, you are explicitly telling that Transport Session is not allowed which also means you will not be using those bindings. Here, most probably you will be using Basic HTTP Binding.

BINDING ENFORCEMENT:-

In order to prove the point TCP Binding works with Transport Session. Let me go ahead and set the session mode to "**NotAllowed**" as shown below in the screen shot.

```
using System;
using System.Collect ([SessionMode SessionMode], [Type CallbackContract], [string ConfigurationName], [string Name], [string Namespace], [ProtectionLevel
using System.Service ProtectionLevel])

                      Initializes a new instance of the ServiceContractAttribute class.
namespace MovieLib.C  SessionMode: Gets or sets whether sessions are allowed, not allowed or required.A SessionMode that indicates whether sessions are
{                     allowed, not allowed, or required.The value is not one of the SessionMode values.
    [ServiceContract(SessionMode = SessionMode.)]
    8 references                                    Allowed
    public interface IMovieService                  NotAllowed
    {                                               Required
        [OperationContract]
        7 references  0/2 passing
        IEnumerable<MovieData> GetDirectorNames();
    }
}
```

With the above change in place when I build and run the app; my app blows app and exception message clearly says that contract binding does not support that.

Pragmatic WCF

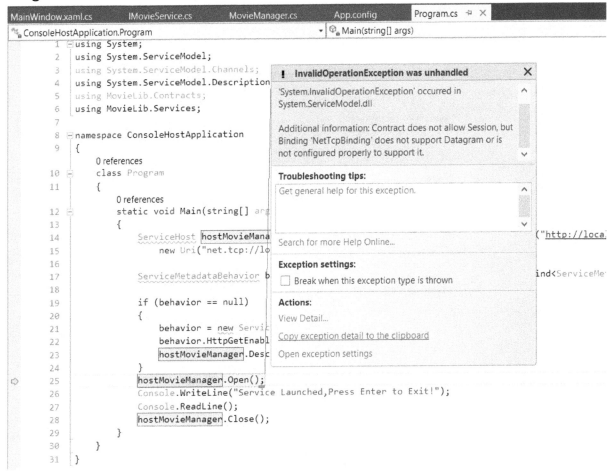

In addition, if you do the same thing reverse means when you set the session mode to
"**Required**" and change the binding to Basic HTTP Binding in endpoint then also it will blow up.

Pragmatic WCF

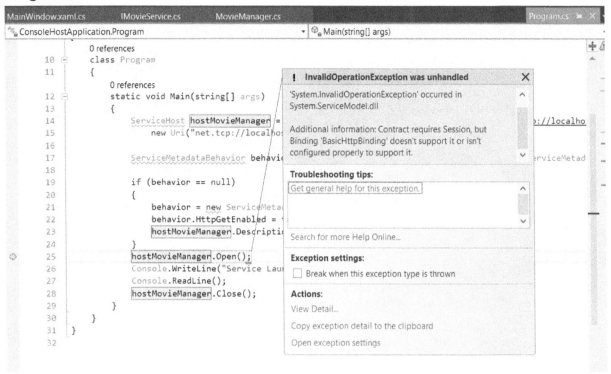

Therefore, you see you have a lot of control when you decide to write session for services, you have a lot of control when you want to enforce your services to be session compatible.

CONCURRENCY:-

Concurrency in WCF determines how a service handles locking during multiple concurrent calls. Now, concurrency in WCF provides three modes. They are-

- Single (default)
- Multiple
- Re-entrant

SINGLE CONCURRENCY:-

Single Concurrency means that the instance of a service is going to allow one call at a time from each proxy. Now, one point to note here is this per instance. Therefore, instance mode is quite relevant here. Therefore, in case of Per Call, it will perform the below mentioned options.

Pragmatic WCF

- Each call will be serviced by a brand new instance.
- Clients can use same proxy on multiple threads. Still new instances.
- Service will process one call at a time.

Per Session: -

- Each proxy will be serviced by a brand new instance.
- Clients can make proxy call on multiple threads. Same instance.
- Service will allow only one call at a time.

Single: -

- Any call from anywhere will be serviced by the same instance.
- Service will allow only one call at a time.

We will discuss the same with demo later in this chapter.

MULTIPLE CONCURRENCY:-

In the case of Multiple Concurrency, WCF stays out of business and provides no locking. It does not prevent multiple clients coming at the same time. Moreover, this can be a deadlock situation depending on different scenarios. Therefore, you must provide your own explicit locking. Therefore, in case of Per Call, it will perform the below mentioned options.

- Each call will be serviced by a brand new instance.
- Clients can use same proxy on multiple threads. Still new instances.
- All calls processed concurrently. No locking needed.

Per Session: -

- Each proxy will be serviced by a brand new instance.
- Clients can make proxy call on multiple threads. Same instance.
- Here, locking rule applies as calls allowed concurrently.

Pragmatic WCF

Single: -

- Any call from anywhere will be serviced by the same instance.
- All calls allowed even from different clients, hence locking rule applies.

RE-ENTRANT CONCURRENCY:-

Re-Entrant concurrency sometimes can be very confusing. It is very similar to single concurrency where it does put lock on the service. Nevertheless, the difference is WCF will ignore the lock if the client will try to access the same one that placed it originally. This is the case when callbacks are needed. Callbacks will call back to the client and possibly return to the service. With these little briefings let us start demo.

CLIENT CODE SETUP:-

First thing I have done here is added the reference for **System.Windows.Forms** namespace so that I can have **messagebox** in my project. Now, the reason I need messagebox not the **console.WriteLine** because I need service to stop in between the process until I press ok on the message box. So, as you can see in the below screen shot I have added the reference in my services project and also modified the service code.

Pragmatic WCF

```
▲ C# MovieLib.Services
  ▷ 🔧 Properties
  ▲ ■·■ References
          ■·■ EntityFramework
          ■·■ EntityFramework.SqlServer
          ■·■ Microsoft.CSharp
          ■·■ MovieLib.Contracts
          ■·■ MovieLib.Core
          ■·■ MovieLib.Data
          ■·■ System
          ■·■ System.ComponentModel.DataAnnotations
          ■·■ System.Core
          ■·■ System.Data
          ■·■ System.Data.DataSetExtensions
          ■·■ System.Runtime.Serialization
          ■·■ System.ServiceModel
          ▣▢ System.Windows.Forms
          ■·■ System.Xml
          ■·■ System.Xml.Linq
      🗍 App.config
  ▷ C# MovieManager.cs
      🗍 packages.config
```

```csharp
using System;

using System.Collections;

using System.Collections.Generic;

using System.Globalization;

using System.Linq;

using System.ServiceModel;

using System.Threading;

using System.Windows.Forms;

using MovieLib.Contracts;

using MovieLib.Data.Entities;

using MovieLib.Data.Repositories;

using MovieLib.Data.Repository_Interfaces;


namespace MovieLib.Services

{

    [ServiceBehavior(InstanceContextMode = InstanceContextMode.PerCall)]
```

Pragmatic WCF

```csharp
    public class MovieManager : IMovieService
{
    private IMovieRepository _iMovieRepository;
    private int _counter = 0;
    public MovieManager()
    {


    }


    public MovieManager(IMovieRepository iMovieRepository)
    {
        _iMovieRepository = iMovieRepository;
    }
    public IEnumerable<MovieData> GetDirectorNames()
    {


        List<MovieData> movieData = new List<MovieData>();


        try
        {
            IMovieRepository movieRepository = _iMovieRepository ?? new
MovieRepository();


            IEnumerable<Movie> movies = movieRepository.GetMovies();


            if (movies != null)
            {
                foreach (Movie movie in movies)
                {
                    movieData.Add(new MovieData()
                    {
                        DirectorName = movie.DirectorName
                    });
                }
            }
            _counter++;
```

Pragmatic WCF

```csharp
            //Console.WriteLine("Counter:- {0}",_counter);

            MessageBox.Show("Counter:-" +_counter);

        }


        catch (Exception ex)
        {
            string.Format("Something messed up - {0}", ex.Message);
        }
        return movieData;

    }

  }

}
```

Now, the next thing, which I am going to change here, is adjust the client. Earlier here we have the standard call on a single thread at the click event of Button and I have class wide variable for proxy. Therefore, now what I do is change the code so that it will make the call on the background thread.

```csharp
using System;
using System.Collections;
using System.Collections.Generic;
using System.ServiceModel;
using System.ServiceModel.Channels;
using System.Threading;
using System.Windows;
using MovieLib.Client.Contracts;
using MovieLib.Client.ServiceReference1;
using MovieLib.Contracts;
using MovieLib.Proxies;


namespace MovieLib.Client
{
    /// <summary>
    /// Interaction logic for MainWindow.xaml
```

Pragmatic WCF

```csharp
        /// </summary>

    public partial class MainWindow : Window
    {
        private MovieClient proxyClient = null;
        private SynchronizationContext synchronizationContext = null;
        public MainWindow()
        {
            InitializeComponent();
            proxyClient = new MovieClient("1stEP");
            synchronizationContext = SynchronizationContext.Current;
        }



        private void Button_Click(object sender, RoutedEventArgs e)
        {
            // MovieClient proxyClient = new MovieClient("1stEP");


            try
            {
                Thread thread = new Thread(() =>
                {
                    IEnumerable<MovieData> data = proxyClient.GetDirectorNames();
                    if (data != null)
                    {
                        SendOrPostCallback callback = new SendOrPostCallback(arg =>
                        {
                            LstDirectors.ItemsSource = data;
                        });
                        synchronizationContext.Send(callback,true);
                    }


                    //   proxyClient.Close();
                });


                thread.IsBackground = true;
```

Pragmatic WCF

```
                thread.Start();
        }
        catch (Exception ex)
        {
            MessageBox.Show("Exception thrown by service." + ex);
        }
    }


    private void Button_Click_1(object sender, RoutedEventArgs e)
    {
        EndpointAddress address = new
EndpointAddress("net.tcp://localhost:8010/MovieService");
        Binding binding = new NetTcpBinding();


        MovieClient proxyClient = new MovieClient(binding, address);


        IEnumerable<MovieData> data = proxyClient.GetDirectorNames();


        if (data != null)
        {
            LstDirectors.ItemsSource = data;
        }


        proxyClient.Close();
    }


    private void btnInvoke_Click(object sender, RoutedEventArgs e)
    {
        EndpointAddress address = new
EndpointAddress("net.tcp://localhost:8011/MovieName");
        Binding binding = new NetTcpBinding();


        ChannelFactory<IMovieName> factory = new ChannelFactory<IMovieName>(binding,
address);


        //ChannelFactory<IMovieName> factory = new ChannelFactory<IMovieName>("");
```

Pragmatic WCF

```
        IMovieName proxy = factory.CreateChannel();


        string value = txtMovieName.Text;
        proxy.ShowMovie(value);


        factory.Close();
    }


    private void Button_Click_2(object sender, RoutedEventArgs e)
    {
        MovieServiceClient proxy = new MovieServiceClient();


        IEnumerable<MovieData> datas = proxy.GetDirectorNames();


        if (datas != null)
        {
            LstDirectors.ItemsSource = datas;
        }


        proxy.Close();


    }


    }
}
```

Now, let me explain the code a bit. As you can see that, I have wrapped all the things inside the button click in a thread, then set the same as background thread, and start the same. I have also introduced the synchronization context. This concept we have already discussed. Because here, we are trying to update the UI but I am in a background thread. Therefore, this will blow up. Hence, to fix the same I have also introduced marshalling which we have already seen in threading topic.

PER CALL TEST:-

One more piece I want to include as I am testing single concurrency here in the service that is setting the concurrency mode to single concurrency.

Pragmatic WCF

```
[ServiceBehavior(InstanceContextMode = InstanceContextMode.PerCall, ConcurrencyMode =
ConcurrencyMode.Single)]
```

Now, when I build and run the app. You will notice that as soon as clicked on Get Directors, your UI become free for the next call and again I clicked on Get Directors; but neither my counter get refreshed nor I receive the data. Nevertheless, as soon as I clicked on the message box; I get the data on my UI and second call took place. Below is the detailed screen shot for the same.

file:///C:/Rahul/My Experiments/MovieLibWCF/MovieLib/ConsoleHostApplicat...
Service Launched,Press Enter to Exit!

Counter:-1

OK

Pragmatic WCF

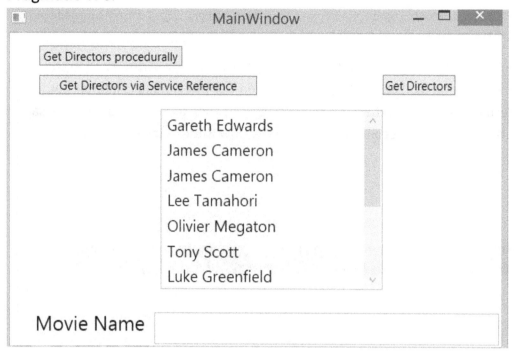

Now, since it was Per Call test for concurrency mode single, hence it will always display the counter as 1. So, even though I am having different instances service is still processing the requests sequentially as I am in single concurrency mode.

PER SESSION TEST:-

Now, let us change the instance mode to Per Session and test the behavior.

```
[ServiceBehavior(InstanceContextMode = InstanceContextMode.PerSession, ConcurrencyMode = ConcurrencyMode.Single)]
```

When I build and run the app, I will see that counter starts getting incremented.

file:///C:/Rahul/My Experiments/MovieLibWCF/MovieLib/ConsoleHostApplicat...

Service Launched,Press Enter to Exit!

Pragmatic WCF

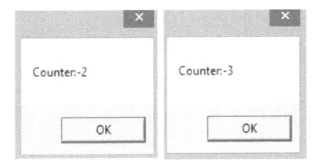

Pragmatic WCF

Therefore, as you can see that concurrency mode and proxy is shared. Hence, counters are getting incremented.

SINGLETON TEST:-

Let us change the context mode to singleton and build the app first.

```
[ServiceBehavior(InstanceContextMode = InstanceContextMode.Single, ConcurrencyMode =
ConcurrencyMode.Single)]
```

Now, let us run two versions of UI means one from Visual Studio and another from bin directory of client. Therefore, when you run the app you will still see that counters are getting incremented but again sequentially which is thread safe.

file:///C:/Rahul/My Experiments/MovieLibWCF/MovieLib/ConsoleHostApplicat...
Service Launched,Press Enter to Exit!

Pragmatic WCF

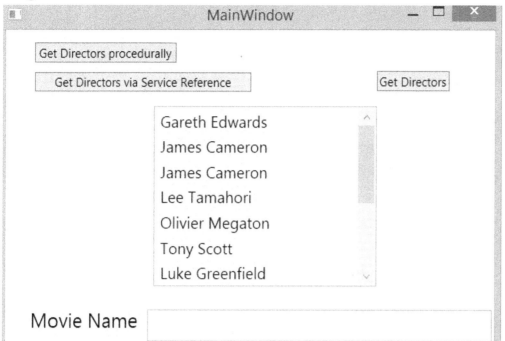

Pragmatic WCF

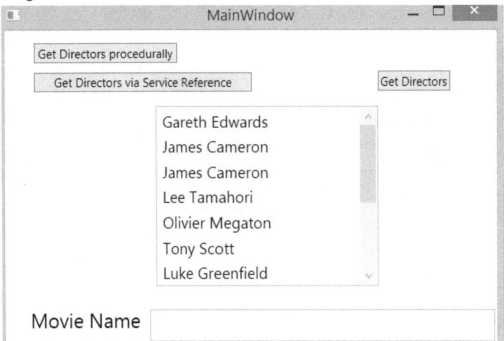

PER CALL MULTIPLE TEST:-

Now, I am going to change the instance Mode back to Per Call and concurrency mode to Multiple. Therefore, effectively I am telling WCF do not become hurdle for me just free me.

```
[ServiceBehavior(InstanceContextMode = InstanceContextMode.PerCall, ConcurrencyMode = ConcurrencyMode.Multiple)]
```

One more change I need to do on the client side is setting the thread affinity. This is because we are dealing with multiple concurrency now. If I do not do that; as soon proxy is opened it will belong to the background thread and this will return wrong result. Hence, I need to simulate

Pragmatic WCF

the proxy call by opening the proxy first. below; in the snippet, I have opened the proxy from the foreground thread.

```
public MainWindow()
    {
        InitializeComponent();
        proxyClient = new MovieClient("1stEP");
        proxyClient.Open();
        synchronizationContext = SynchronizationContext.Current;
    }
```

With the above change in place, now the proxy belongs to this thread. When I build and run the app, then it will produce me the concurrent results. As you can see below in the screen shot; when I clicked Get Directors first, it gave me counter one. Then I again clicked on Get Directors, it again gave me a different message box but with counter one itself as this per call. Now, when I clicked individually on these message boxes, it returned me results.

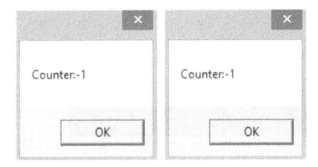

Pragmatic WCF

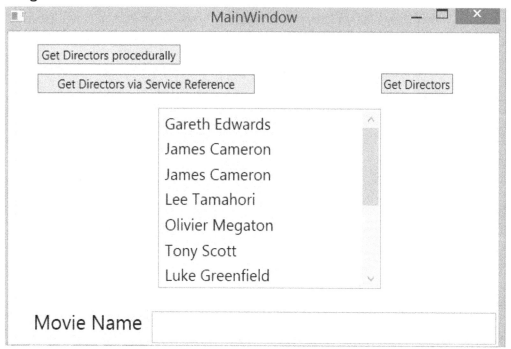

PER SESSION MULTIPLE TEST:-

Let us set the context mode to Per Session and then test the same.

```
[ServiceBehavior(InstanceContextMode = InstanceContextMode.PerSession, ConcurrencyMode =
ConcurrencyMode.Multiple)]
```

I am quite sure by this time you would have guessed its output. Even then, let us build the app and test again.

```
file:///C:/Rahul/My Experiments/MovieLibWCF/MovieLib/ConsoleHostApplicat...
Service Launched,Press Enter to Exit!
```

Pragmatic WCF

Therefore, as you can see in the above screen shot, all these calls are happening concurrently but since proxy is shared, hence counters are getting incremented.

Pragmatic WCF

SINGLETON MULTIPLE TEST:-

Let us set the context mode to single and then test the behavior.

```
[ServiceBehavior(InstanceContextMode = InstanceContextMode.Single, ConcurrencyMode =
ConcurrencyMode.Multiple)]
```

Again, since this is singleton test, I would be running two versions of client. Moreover, this will produce me the below result.

file:///C:/Rahul/My Experiments/MovieLibWCF/MovieLib/ConsoleHostApplicat...
Service Launched,Press Enter to Exit!

Pragmatic WCF

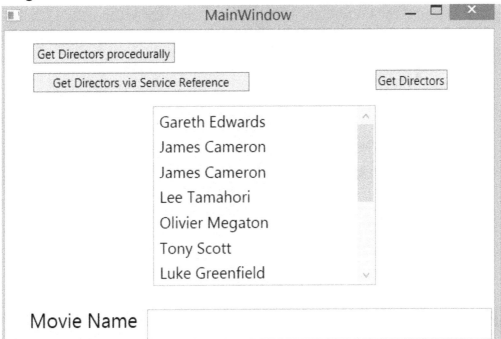

Pragmatic WCF

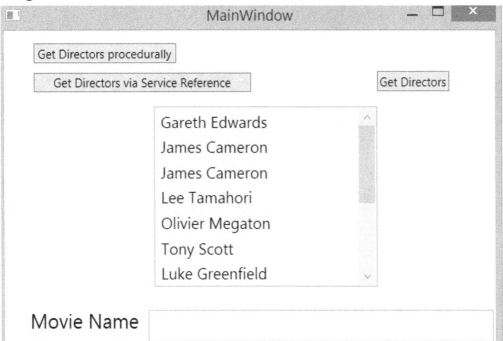

TASK TEST:-

In this section, I am going to modify my client code. Therefore, instead of using thread here; I will use Task and off course will use Thread Pool to achieve the same thing. So, as you can see the below snippet I have used **await Task.Run** and wrapped my entire code there. Moreover, you cannot await until its **async** method.

```
private async void Button_Click(object sender, RoutedEventArgs e)
    {
        // MovieClient proxyClient = new MovieClient("1stEP");
```

Pragmatic WCF

```
try
{
    await Task.Run(() =>
    {
        IEnumerable<MovieData> data = proxyClient.GetDirectorNames();
        if (data != null)
        {
            SendOrPostCallback callback = (arg =>
            {
                LstDirectors.ItemsSource = data;
            });
            synchronizationContext.Send(callback,true);
        }


        //   proxyClient.Close();
    });


}
catch (Exception ex)
{
    MessageBox.Show("Exception thrown by service." + ex);
}
}
```

With the above changes in place when, I run the same it will produce me the same behavior what we tested initially.

SUMMARY:-

In this section, we have seen variety of techniques to achieve instancing and concurrency. We started this chapter with the discussion on different modes of instancing. We then, tested their behavior individually. Then, we have jumped into concurrency section. Here, also we have seen three different modes with different context modes. In the next section, we will discuss more on Exception handling.

Pragmatic WCF

WHAT DO you find in this CHAPTER?

- Introduction
- SOAP Faults
- Scenario 1
- Scenario 2
- Unhandled Exception
- Unhandled Exception – 2nd
- Unhandled Exception – 3rd
- Handle Fault Exception
- Handle Fault Exception of T
- Handle with Custom Contract
- Summary

INTRODUCTION:-

I think one of the most important chapters for any topic is Exception Handling. I have seen that many developers tend to skip exception handling. Means they usually do not take this seriously. But, in case of WCF, this is really important because in a conventional system we have services hosted in one machine, clients sitting on another machine, error thrown by one captured by other. So, let us get started by discussing SOAP Faults.

SOAP FAULTS:-

By default CLR, exceptions cannot cross machine boundaries. Nevertheless, SOAP being in the middle and WCF helping SOAP; this is actually possible to simulate. Hence, WCF actually uses SOAP faults. Here, what we need to do is to turn the exception into a SOAP fault and then WCF will reverse the process back at the client. Therefore, **SOAP Fault is a specification defining fault message that is packaged and passed from service to client**. Now, the best thing here is WCF provides a .NET Programming model to accommodate this without knowing anything about this. Therefore, in case of SOAP Faults, series of things happen.

Pragmatic WCF

- Service throws exception.
- WCF packages it as a SOAP fault, embeds it in response message.
- Client recreates received SOAP faults as CLR exception and throws it
- Then client proxy code can be wrapped in a standard Try-Catch call

SCENARIO 1:-

First scenario, which I am going to talk here, is the unhandled exception means you just let the exception to occur. In this particular case what happens; service behavior "**IncludeException DetailsInFault**" is set to **false**. This also means client will only receive **Fault Exception**. In this case, client will not catch anything else. Only thing which client will catch is base exception with no additional information. One more important point to note here, that any unhandled exception occurs, in that case proxy is faulted, which means proxy cannot be reused.

Now, exact same scenario can be reproduced by turning "**IncludeException DetailsInFault**" set to true. Here, in this case following things will happen.

- Client receives **FaultException<ExceptionDetail>**
- Can read exception message
- Can read original exception type.
- Proxy faulted.

Therefore, here FaultException<T> is a derivative of FaultException. Now, setting this to true, you can have additional information coming out of the service. Therefore, inside the exception variable say **ex**, you will be having inner details of the root cause. In this case, also, proxy is still faulted means you cannot reuse proxy. One more point to note here, that service behavior can be set from the config as well.

SCENARIO 2:-

The next scenario, which I believe, is the minimum one, which you should have in your service. Moreover, this is where you setup your service to catch the expected exceptions and re-throw the same as a fault exception. Here, client can read the message, which you have put while re-throwing the same. Part that is more important is you can reuse the proxy, as proxy is not

Pragmatic WCF

faulted in this case. Nevertheless, one point which you should remember here that client could catch only one type of exception here.

Now, consider the below mentioned behavior.

- FaultException<T> thrown
- Client receives FaultException<T>
- You can read complete exception message
- Proxy can be reused
- T here can be exception or custom fault contract

Therefore, in this case client will have the ultimate power in catching multiple type of exceptions.

UNHANDLED EXCEPTION:-

Below I have pasted one snippet from Movie Manager Class. Let me explain the code a bit, here I am throwing a plain CLR exception. Now, this scenario is considered an unhandled exception. Reason is if it is not a fault exception, WCF will treat any non-fault exception an unhandled exception that WCF does not know what to do with Non-Fault exception. It will remain considered unhandled.

```
public IEnumerable<MovieData> GetDirectorNames()
    {
        List<MovieData> movieData = new List<MovieData>();

            IMovieRepository movieRepository = _iMovieRepository ?? new
MovieRepository();

            IEnumerable<Movie> movies = movieRepository.GetMovies();

    if (movies.Count() != 0)
        {
        foreach (Movie movie in movies)
        {
            movieData.Add(new MovieData()
```

Pragmatic WCF

```
            {
                    DirectorName = movie.DirectorName
            });
        }
    }
    else
    {
        throw new Exception("List is empty");
    }

        _counter++;
        //Console.WriteLine("Counter:- {0}",_counter);
        MessageBox.Show("Counter:-" +_counter);


        return movieData;
    }
```

Then, in the client side, I have also included the try catch section to ensure that we see exact message. In addition, I have changed the project setting for console host, so that it will run out side of debugging mode.

```
private async void Button_Click(object sender, RoutedEventArgs e)
    {
        try
        {
            await Task.Run(() =>
            {
                IEnumerable<MovieData> data = proxyClient.GetDirectorNames();
                if (data != null)
                {
                    SendOrPostCallback callback = (arg =>
                    {
                        LstDirectors.ItemsSource = data;
                    });
                    synchronizationContext.Send(callback,true);
```

Pragmatic WCF

```
                }


        });


    }
    catch (Exception ex)
    {
        MessageBox.Show("Exception thrown by service.\n\r" + ex+
            ex.GetType().Name+"\n\r"+
            "Message:-" + ex.Message + "\n\r"+
            "Proxy State:- " + proxyClient.State.ToString());
    }
}
```

Now, with the above change in place, when I go ahead and run the app. Then, in that case it will produce me the below shown result.

Pragmatic WCF

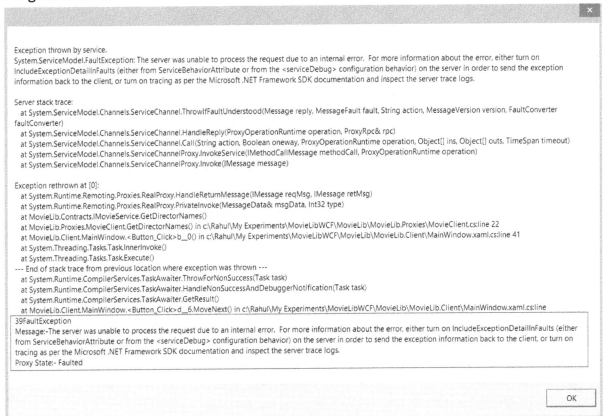

Therefore, as you can see in the above screen shot; there is actually nothing to show here. Moreover, proxy state is faulted. Therefore, if you tries to use the proxy then it will fail. Hence, you need to completely new up the proxy or in other words recycle the same to use again.

UNHANDLED EXCEPTION – 2ND:-

Now, in this case, I will come to movie manager class and turn the behavior to true so that I can receive the actual fault message at client side.

```
[ServiceBehavior(IncludeExceptionDetailInFaults = true)]
```

With the above change in place when I go ahead and run the same again, this will produce me the below error message.

Pragmatic WCF

As you can see in the above screen shot, it gave my custom error. Nevertheless, proxy is still faulted. In addition, when you see the above screen shot, it is producing the type of exception as well. However, to be specific let us catch the type of the exception as well.

Pragmatic WCF

UNHANDLED EXCEPTION – 3RD:-

In this section, I will go ahead and modify the client code as shown below in snippet. Let me explain the code a bit. Here, I have included another catch to catch the FaultException<T> and wrapped the same in detail property.

```csharp
private async void Button_Click(object sender, RoutedEventArgs e)
    {
        // MovieClient proxyClient = new MovieClient("1stEP");


        try
        {
            await Task.Run(() =>
            {
                IEnumerable<MovieData> data = proxyClient.GetDirectorNames();
                if (data != null)
                {
                    SendOrPostCallback callback = (arg =>
                    {
                        LstDirectors.ItemsSource = data;
                    });
                    synchronizationContext.Send(callback, true);
                }


                //   proxyClient.Close();
            });


        }
        catch (FaultException<ExceptionDetail> ex)
        {
            MessageBox.Show("Exception thrown by service.\n\r Exception Type:-" + ex
+
                "Message:-" + ex.Detail.Message + "\n\r" +
                "Proxy State:- " + proxyClient.State);
        }
        catch (Exception ex)
```

Pragmatic WCF

```
        {
            MessageBox.Show("Exception thrown by service.\n\r Exception Type:-" + ex+
                ex.GetType().Name+"\n\r"+
                "Message:-" + ex.Message + "\n\r"+
                "Proxy State:- " + proxyClient.State);
        }
    }
```

Now, let us try to run the same. Upon, running it produced me the below behavior.

Pragmatic WCF

However, there is no difference between with the previous one. However, you can handle the same in a cleaner and simpler way.

Pragmatic WCF

HANDLE FAULT EXCEPTION:-

In this section, we will see more about Handled Exception. Therefore, here in Movie Manager Class rather than throwing simple exception, I will throw Fault Exception as shown below in the snippet.

```
throw new FaultException("List is empty");
```

In addition, back in the client side I can say like

```
private async void Button_Click(object sender, RoutedEventArgs e)
        {
          // MovieClient proxyClient = new MovieClient("1stEP");

          try
          {
              await Task.Run(() =>
              {
                  IEnumerable<MovieData> data = proxyClient.GetDirectorNames();
                  if (data != null)
                  {
                      SendOrPostCallback callback = (arg =>
                      {
                          LstDirectors.ItemsSource = data;
                      });
                      synchronizationContext.Send(callback, true);
                  }

                  //   proxyClient.Close();
              });

          }
          catch (FaultException<ExceptionDetail> ex)
          {
              MessageBox.Show("Exception thrown by service.\n\r Exception Type:-" + ex
```

+

Pragmatic WCF

```
                    "Message:-" + ex.Detail.Message + "\n\r" +

                    "Proxy State:- " + proxyClient.State);

            }
            catch (FaultException ex)

            {

                MessageBox.Show("Fault Exception thrown by service.\n\r Exception Type:-"
+ ex +

                    "Message:-" + ex.Message + "\n\r" +

                    "Proxy State:- " + proxyClient.State);

            }
            catch (Exception ex)

            {

                MessageBox.Show("Exception thrown by service.\n\r Exception Type:-" + ex+

                    ex.GetType().Name+"\n\r"+

                    "Message:-" + ex.Message + "\n\r"+

                    "Proxy State:- " + proxyClient.State);

            }

        }
```

Therefore, here I have added another catch block for Fault Exception with the same detail. Nevertheless, let us check the output now.

Pragmatic WCF

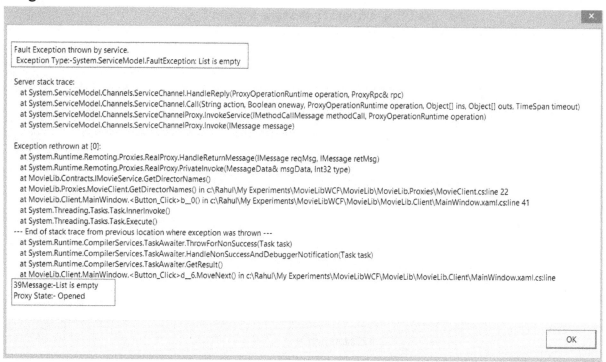

```
Fault Exception thrown by service.
Exception Type:-System.ServiceModel.FaultException: List is empty

Server stack trace:
    at System.ServiceModel.Channels.ServiceChannel.HandleReply(ProxyOperationRuntime operation, ProxyRpc& rpc)
    at System.ServiceModel.Channels.ServiceChannel.Call(String action, Boolean oneway, ProxyOperationRuntime operation, Object[] ins, Object[] outs, TimeSpan timeout)
    at System.ServiceModel.Channels.ServiceChannelProxy.InvokeService(IMethodCallMessage methodCall, ProxyOperationRuntime operation)
    at System.ServiceModel.Channels.ServiceChannelProxy.Invoke(IMessage message)

Exception rethrown at [0]:
    at System.Runtime.Remoting.Proxies.RealProxy.HandleReturnMessage(IMessage reqMsg, IMessage retMsg)
    at System.Runtime.Remoting.Proxies.RealProxy.PrivateInvoke(MessageData& msgData, Int32 type)
    at MovieLib.Contracts.IMovieService.GetDirectorNames()
    at MovieLib.Proxies.MovieClient.GetDirectorNames() in c:\Rahul\My Experiments\MovieLibWCF\MovieLib\MovieLib.Proxies\MovieClient.cs:line 22
    at MovieLib.Client.MainWindow.<Button_Click>b__0() in c:\Rahul\My Experiments\MovieLibWCF\MovieLib\MovieLib.Client\MainWindow.xaml.cs:line 41
    at System.Threading.Tasks.Task.InnerInvoke()
    at System.Threading.Tasks.Task.Execute()
--- End of stack trace from previous location where exception was thrown ---
    at System.Runtime.CompilerServices.TaskAwaiter.ThrowForNonSuccess(Task task)
    at System.Runtime.CompilerServices.TaskAwaiter.HandleNonSuccessAndDebuggerNotification(Task task)
    at System.Runtime.CompilerServices.TaskAwaiter.GetResult()
    at MovieLib.Client.MainWindow.<Button_Click>d__6.MoveNext() in c:\Rahul\My Experiments\MovieLibWCF\MovieLib\MovieLib.Client\MainWindow.xaml.cs:line
39Message:-List is empty
Proxy State:- Opened
```

`OK`

As you can see in the above screen, shot that **state** is still **open** which means it can be reutilized for doing further processing. Now, let us look the same with more detail.

HANDLE FAULT EXCEPTION OF T:-

In this section, we will see how to throw application exception to the client. During this course I will do couple of thing at the service side. Below is the snippet for the Movie Manager class.

```
public IEnumerable<MovieData> GetDirectorNames()
    {

        List<MovieData> movieData = new List<MovieData>();


        IMovieRepository movieRepository = _iMovieRepository ?? new
MovieRepository();


        IEnumerable<Movie> movies = movieRepository.GetMovies();
```

Pragmatic WCF

```csharp
            if (movies.Count() != 0)
            {
                foreach (Movie movie in movies)
                {
                    movieData.Add(new MovieData()
                    {
                        DirectorName = movie.DirectorName
                    });
                }
            }
            else
            {
                //throw new Exception("List is empty");
                // throw new FaultException("List is empty");
                ApplicationException ex = new ApplicationException("List is empty");

                throw new FaultException<ApplicationException>(ex,"Wrong DB instance");
            }
                _counter++;
                //Console.WriteLine("Counter:- {0}",_counter);
                MessageBox.Show("Counter:-" +_counter);



        return movieData;
    }


using System;
using System.Collections.Generic;
using System.ServiceModel;


namespace MovieLib.Contracts
{
    [ServiceContract]
    public interface IMovieService
```

Pragmatic WCF

```
        {
            [OperationContract]
            [FaultContract(typeof(ApplicationException))]
            IEnumerable<MovieData> GetDirectorNames();
        }
    }
```

Now, let me go ahead and explain the code a bit. As you can see that, I have created one new instance of application exception and then I have passed my custom message to it and then thrown the Fault Exception. However, in order to receive this application exception at client side; I have to include the same in the Fault contract as well. This is how I tell the serializer that it need to serialize the application exception and send the same across the wire. Therefore, you need to do this for every **FaultException<T>**. Now, let us make the change at client side. Below is the snippet for the same.

```
private async void Button_Click(object sender, RoutedEventArgs e)
        {
          // MovieClient proxyClient = new MovieClient("1stEP");

            try
            {
                await Task.Run(() =>
                {
                    IEnumerable<MovieData> data = proxyClient.GetDirectorNames();
                    if (data != null)
                    {
                        SendOrPostCallback callback = (arg =>
                        {
                            LstDirectors.ItemsSource = data;
                        });
                        synchronizationContext.Send(callback, true);
                    }

                    //   proxyClient.Close();
                });
```

Pragmatic WCF

```csharp
                }
                catch (FaultException<ExceptionDetail> ex)
                {
                    MessageBox.Show("Exception thrown by service.\n\r Exception Type:-" + ex
+
                        "Message:-" + ex.Detail.Message + "\n\r" +
                        "Proxy State:- " + proxyClient.State);
                }


                catch (FaultException<ApplicationException> ex)
                {
                    MessageBox.Show("Exception thrown by
FaultException<ApplicationException>.\n\r Exception Type:-" + ex +
                        "Message:-" + ex.Detail.Message + "\n\r" +
                        "Proxy State:- " + proxyClient.State);
                }


                catch (FaultException ex)
                {
                    MessageBox.Show("Fault Exception thrown by service.\n\r Exception Type:-"
+ ex +
                        "Message:-" + ex.Message + "\n\r" +
                        "Proxy State:- " + proxyClient.State);
                }
                catch (Exception ex)
                {
                    MessageBox.Show("Exception thrown by service.\n\r Exception Type:-" + ex+
                        ex.GetType().Name+"\n\r"+
                        "Message:-" + ex.Message + "\n\r"+
                        "Proxy State:- " + proxyClient.State);
                }
            }
```

Pragmatic WCF

Now, one more thing to note here is that ordering of catch block is very important otherwise, it will not catch. Therefore, the thumb rule is; parent class has to come at last. With this change in place, let us go ahead build the app and see the result.

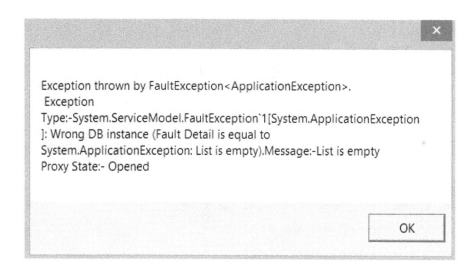

Exception thrown by FaultException<ApplicationException>.
 Exception
Type:-System.ServiceModel.FaultException`1[System.ApplicationException
]: Wrong DB instance (Fault Detail is equal to
System.ApplicationException: List is empty).Message:-List is empty
Proxy State:- Opened

OK

HANDLE WITH CUSTOM CONTRACT:-

This one is my personal favorite. Here, I have created my one custom class as shown below in the Contracts project.

```
using System.Runtime.Serialization;

namespace MovieLib.Contracts
{
```

Pragmatic WCF

```
    [DataContract]
  public class DataNotFound
  {
        [DataMember]
        public string Message { get; set; }


        [DataMember]
        public string When { get; set; }


        [DataMember]
        public string User { get; set; }



    }
}
```

Above snippet is custom data contract. This is very flexible; it entirely depends on you what information's you would like to grab here. You can also put one string to catch the complete stack trace apart from regular stuffs.

```
public IEnumerable<MovieData> GetDirectorNames()
    {

        List<MovieData> movieData = new List<MovieData>();


            IMovieRepository movieRepository = _iMovieRepository ?? new
MovieRepository();


            IEnumerable<Movie> movies = movieRepository.GetMovies();

        if (movies.Count() != 0)
        {
            foreach (Movie movie in movies)
            {
                movieData.Add(new MovieData()
```

Pragmatic WCF

```
                {
                        DirectorName = movie.DirectorName
                });
            }
        }
        else
        {
            DataNotFound ex = new DataNotFound()
            {
                Message = "Data Not Found",
                When = DateTime.Now.ToString(),
                User = "Rahul"
            };
            throw new FaultException<DataNotFound>(ex,"Custom Exception");
        }
            _counter++;
            //Console.WriteLine("Counter:- {0}",_counter);
            MessageBox.Show("Counter:-" +_counter);



        return movieData;
    }
```

Now, again I need to include the same in the Fault Contract.

```
using System;
using System.Collections.Generic;
using System.ServiceModel;

namespace MovieLib.Contracts
{
    [ServiceContract]
    public interface IMovieService
```

Pragmatic WCF

```csharp
    {
        [OperationContract]
        [FaultContract(typeof(ApplicationException))]
        [FaultContract(typeof(DataNotFound))]
        IEnumerable<MovieData> GetDirectorNames();

    }

}
```

Once service side changes done; I can go ahead and make client side changes as shown below.

```csharp
private async void Button_Click(object sender, RoutedEventArgs e)
        {
            // MovieClient proxyClient = new MovieClient("1stEP");


            try
            {
                await Task.Run(() =>
                {
                    IEnumerable<MovieData> data = proxyClient.GetDirectorNames();
                    if (data != null)
                    {
                        SendOrPostCallback callback = (arg =>
                        {
                            LstDirectors.ItemsSource = data;
                        });
                        synchronizationContext.Send(callback, true);
                    }


                    //   proxyClient.Close();
                });


            }
            catch (FaultException<ExceptionDetail> ex)
            {
                MessageBox.Show("Exception thrown by service.\n\r Exception Type:-" + ex
+
                    "Message:-" + ex.Detail.Message + "\n\r" +
                    "Proxy State:- " + proxyClient.State);
```

Pragmatic WCF

```csharp
            }


            catch (FaultException<ApplicationException> ex)
            {
                MessageBox.Show("Exception thrown by
FaultException<ApplicationException>.\n\r Exception Type:-" + ex +
                    "Message:-" + ex.Detail.Message + "\n\r" +
                    "Proxy State:- " + proxyClient.State);
            }


            catch (FaultException<DataNotFound> ex)
            {
                MessageBox.Show("Exception thrown by FaultException<DataNotFound>.\n\r
Exception Type:-" + ex +
                    "Message:-" + ex.Detail.Message + "\n\r" +
                    "User:- " + ex.Detail.User + "\n\r" +
                    "When:- " + ex.Detail.When + "\n\r" +
                    "Proxy State:- " + proxyClient.State);
            }


            catch (FaultException ex)
            {
                MessageBox.Show("Fault Exception thrown by service.\n\r Exception Type:-"
+ ex +
                    "Message:-" + ex.Message + "\n\r" +
                    "Proxy State:- " + proxyClient.State);
            }
            catch (Exception ex)
            {
                MessageBox.Show("Exception thrown by service.\n\r Exception Type:-" + ex+
                    ex.GetType().Name+"\n\r"+
                    "Message:-" + ex.Message + "\n\r"+
                    "Proxy State:- " + proxyClient.State);
            }
        }
```

Pragmatic WCF

With the above changes in place, when I go and build the app then it will produce me the detailed view of the exception.

Exception thrown by FaultException<DataNotFound>.
Exception
Type:-System.ServiceModel.FaultException`1[MovieLib.Contracts.DataNotF
ound]: Custom Exception (Fault Detail is equal to
MovieLib.Contracts.DataNotFound).Message:-Data Not Found
User:- Rahul
When:- 5/17/2015 3:24:50 PM
Proxy State:- Opened

OK

Therefore, this is the power of using custom data contract to handle the exception. You can include as many properties as you want.

SUMMARY:-

In this section, we have seen Exception Handling in detail. We have started with a blank slate as in unhandled exception. We first saw how unhandled exceptions can create problems as this will make the proxy defaulted. Then, we also saw how to handle the unhandled exception. Later on, we covered different categories of Handled Exceptions and its behavior. Last but not the least we saw how to handle fault exceptions with variety of techniques.

Pragmatic WCF

CHAPTER 10: OPERATION MANAGEMENT

WHAT DO you find in this CHAPTER?

- Introduction
- Request-Response
- One-Way Operation
- One-Way Coding
- Changing Binding
- Callback Operations
- Callback Implementation
- Clearing Deadlock
- Replacing Message-box
- Using Thread
- Changing Thread to Task
- Summary

INTRODUCTION:-

One of the great and unique way of using WCF, it has several different way of making operation calls. Unlike WEB API, which is again a great technology but it does the operation handling only one-way. With WCF, different types of operations are available that you can invoke. They are-

- Request/Response :-
- One-Way Operations :-
- Callbacks (Duplex Calls) :-
- Async Calls :-

REQUEST-RESPONSE:-

Request-Response calls are the easiest ones. They are standard ones. Whatever, we have done in the WCF design so far is Request-Response example. In SOAP terms, request sent to the service and there is response SOAP message comes from the service. This holds true even for

Pragmatic WCF

Void operations. Even with void operations, response message will be there from service. In this case, client blocks the call until call is complete.

ONE-WAY OPERATIONS:-

One-Way operations are little different. They are considered as fire and forget calls. One-Way operations must have **Void** return type. Reason to have this Void return type because it will not have any SOAP response message. Moreover, because of that there is no support for Fault Handling. They also need to be marked with **IsOneWay** property in operation contract. With one-way operation, when you make a call, you will immediately get the control of the client. Nevertheless, if there is any Transport Session present and proxy gets closed client will remain blocked until call completes.

ONE-WAY CODING:-

Before, jumping to learn one-way coding; let me give you a refresher of request-response implementation. So, let us start with contract section.

```csharp
using System;
using System.Collections.Generic;
using System.ServiceModel;

namespace MovieLib.Contracts
{
    [ServiceContract]
    public interface IMovieService
    {
        [OperationContract]
        [FaultContract(typeof(ApplicationException))]
        [FaultContract(typeof(DataNotFound))]
        IEnumerable<MovieData> GetDirectorNames();

        [OperationContract]
        void OneWayOperation();
```

Pragmatic WCF

```
    }
}
```

In the above snippet, I have added one Operation Contract with the name **"OneWayOperation"** and implemented the same thing in service as shown below.

```csharp
public void OneWayOperation()
{
    MessageBox.Show("Hello From Service");
}
```

Once, service side changes done; then we need to implement the same on client side for channel changes.

```csharp
using System.ServiceModel;
using System.ServiceModel.Channels;
using MovieLib.Contracts;
using System.Collections.Generic;

namespace MovieLib.Proxies
{
    public class MovieClient : ClientBase<IMovieService>, IMovieService
    {
        public MovieClient(string endpointName):base(endpointName)
        {

        }

        public MovieClient(Binding binding,EndpointAddress address):base(binding,address)
        {

        }
        public IEnumerable<MovieData> GetDirectorNames()
```

Pragmatic WCF

```
        {
            return Channel.GetDirectorNames();
        }


        public void OneWayOperation()
        {
            Channel.OneWayOperation();
        }
    }
}
```

Last but not the least is the XAML changes with proxy initiation and invocation.

```
private void Button_Click_3(object sender, RoutedEventArgs e)
        {
            MovieClient proxy = new MovieClient("1stEP");
            proxy.OneWayOperation();
            MessageBox.Show("Hello From client");
            proxy.Close();
        }
```

Now, when I run the same; I will first receive the message from the service message box and then it will come to the client and lastly after completion of job gracefully closes the proxy.

Pragmatic WCF

Pragmatic WCF

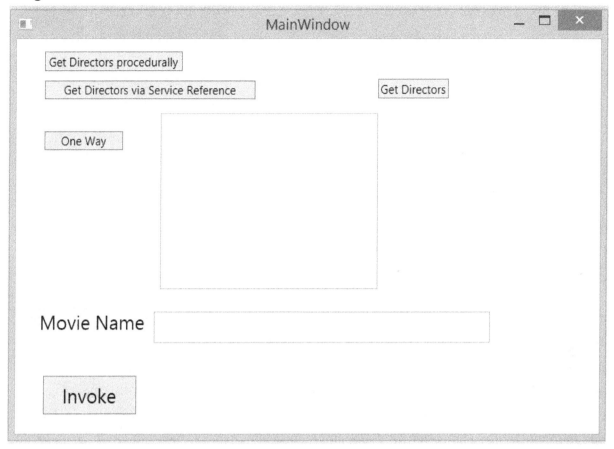

Pragmatic WCF

Now, during this entire process, I cannot get the access to the client, as this is request-response type. Now, let us go ahead and make the same one-way process.

```
[OperationContract(IsOneWay=true)]
        void OneWayOperation();
```

Now, with the above change in place, when I go ahead and run the app, I will get the control back as soon as I invoke the first call. Now, let me explain one more point here. We are using netTcp binding here which means we are using Transport Session. Now, let me go ahead and add another message box after the proxy close.

```
private void Button_Click_3(object sender, RoutedEventArgs e)
        {
            MovieClient proxy = new MovieClient("1stEP");
            proxy.OneWayOperation();
            MessageBox.Show("Hello From client");
            proxy.Close();
            MessageBox.Show("Proxy closed");
        }
```

With the above change in place, when I build and run the app, then it will produce me the below result.

Pragmatic WCF

Now, here if I click on OK in the client window; it will not give me another message immediately. It is still the service, which is holding the same. However, once I click on the service message-box, it will give me another message as shown below.

Hence, if there is Transport Session active; you can make any number of fire and forget call and you will get the control back immediately. Nevertheless, as soon as you hit the proxy closed; it means all the client calls are done and client is blocked. Now, there is a workaround to this as well if that is important to you.

CHANGING BINDING:-

Let us change binding to Basic HTTP Binding both on the client and service side. Below is the snippet for the same and configurations for client and server.

```
private void Button_Click_3(object sender, RoutedEventArgs e)
        {
```

Pragmatic WCF

```
        MovieClient proxy = new MovieClient("2ndEP");

        proxy.OneWayOperation();

        MessageBox.Show("Hello From client");

        proxy.Close();

        MessageBox.Show("Proxy closed");

    }
```

```xml
<endpoint address="http://localhost/MovieService" binding="basicHttpBinding"
        contract="MovieLib.Contracts.IMovieService" name="2ndEP" />
```

```xml
<endpoint address="http://localhost/MovieService"
                binding="basicHttpBinding"
                contract="MovieLib.Contracts.IMovieService"/>
```

With the above change in place, what will happen, now when I click on client message-box, it will simply return the proxy close message first and still remain in the service.

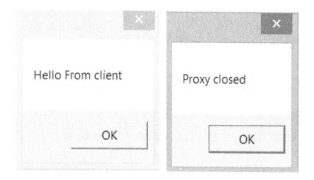

CALLBACK OPERATIONS:-

Callbacks are one of the powerful features of WCF. It is also one of the features, which make WCF stand out from other technologies. Callbacks are also known as Duplex calls. It is an ability for service to call back to the client. The first requirement with Callback is they only work with Net TCP Binding, IPC or WS-HTTP Binding with either reliability or security turned on. In order to setup callbacks; rules are simple. Here, roles are reversed means client becomes service and vice versa temporarily. However, other things like Contracts, Channels will remain the same.

Pragmatic WCF

Now, callbacks are very useful for reporting purpose back to the client. However, while making any callback, certain things need to be taken care:-

- Must consider threading issues.
- Marshalling Issue
- Need to async the call

CALLBACK IMPLEMENTATION:-

In this section, I have made the endpoint as TCP binding because in Callbacks this is one of the requirements. Therefore, what I am going to do here in Movie Manager, inside the loop as soon as it fetches the data from; every time it will notify the client. For that purpose, I will code in that area. Now, let me go ahead and create another service operation as shown below.

```
[ServiceContract]
public interface IUpdateMovieCallback
{
    [OperationContract(IsOneWay = true)]
    void movieCallback();
}
```

Now, the above interface has one method only that I have set to one way. However, there is no dependency as such to have only one-way operation; you can have Request-Response operation as well. This is the service contract, which defines the operation which service is going to use to call back to the client. Now, in order to make the above contract as the callback contract, I need to physically link the contract with the original service contract like shown below.

```
using System;
using System.Collections.Generic;
using System.ServiceModel;

namespace MovieLib.Contracts
{
    [ServiceContract(CallbackContract = typeof(IUpdateMovieCallback))]
    public interface IMovieService
```

Pragmatic WCF

```
    {
        [OperationContract]
        [FaultContract(typeof(ApplicationException))]
        [FaultContract(typeof(DataNotFound))]
        IEnumerable<MovieData> GetDirectorNames();


        [OperationContract(IsOneWay=true)]
        void OneWayOperation();
    }


[ServiceContract]
public interface IUpdateMovieCallback
{
    [OperationContract(IsOneWay = true)]
    void movieCallback();
}
}
```

Now, I need to go in the operations and do the changes. Below I have pasted the snippet for Movie Manager. Now, let me explain the code a bit.

```
public IEnumerable<MovieData> GetDirectorNames()
    {
        List<MovieData> movieData = new List<MovieData>();

            IMovieRepository movieRepository = _iMovieRepository ?? new
MovieRepository();

            IEnumerable<Movie> movies = movieRepository.GetMovies();

        if (movies.Count() != 0)
        {
            foreach (Movie movie in movies)
            {
                movieData.Add(new MovieData()
```

Pragmatic WCF

```csharp
            {
                DirectorName = movie.DirectorName
            });
            //Notify the client
            IUpdateMovieCallback callback =
OperationContext.Current.GetCallbackChannel<IUpdateMovieCallback>();
            if (callback != null)
            {
                callback.movieCallback();
            }
        }


    }
    else
    {
        DataNotFound ex = new DataNotFound()
        {
            Message = "Data Not Found",
            When = DateTime.Now.ToString(),
            User = "Rahul"
        };
        throw new FaultException<DataNotFound>(ex,"Custom Exception");
    }
        _counter++;
        MessageBox.Show("Counter:-" +_counter);


    return movieData;
}
```

Now, the service is temporarily client it is going to need proxy. Nevertheless, we are not going to create an actual proxy class rather we will use channel factory to obtain the proxy. Therefore, operation context of the service call has information about the client. Then, in the callback section, I have called the method **movieCallBack,** which is there in the client side; I will explain that later. Here, service side changes are done. Nevertheless, we have not done yet. We still have to do many client side changes. Below, I have pasted the client side changes.

Pragmatic WCF

```csharp
using System.ServiceModel;
using System.ServiceModel.Channels;
using MovieLib.Contracts;
using System.Collections.Generic;

namespace MovieLib.Proxies
{
    public class MovieClient : DuplexClientBase<IMovieService>, IMovieService
    {
        public MovieClient(string endpointName):base(endpointName)
        {

        }


        public MovieClient(InstanceContext instanceContext, Binding binding,
EndpointAddress address)
            : base(instanceContext,binding, address)
        {

        }
        public IEnumerable<MovieData> GetDirectorNames()
        {
            return Channel.GetDirectorNames();
        }

        public void OneWayOperation()
        {
            Channel.OneWayOperation();
        }
    }
}
```

Pragmatic WCF

As you can see above, I have changed **ClientBase** to **DuplexClientBase.** In addition, I have changed the constructors' implementation accordingly. Now, let us go ahead and change the desktop implementation of the code. Below I have pasted the change for the same.

```
public void movieCallback()
      {
          MessageBox.Show("Directors Fetched");
      }
      private void Button_Click_1(object sender, RoutedEventArgs e)
      {
          EndpointAddress address = new
EndpointAddress("net.tcp://localhost:8010/MovieService");
          Binding binding = new NetTcpBinding();

          MovieClient proxyClient = new MovieClient(new
InstanceContext(this),binding,address);
          //MovieClient proxyClient = new MovieClient(binding, address);

          IEnumerable<MovieData> data = proxyClient.GetDirectorNames();

          if (data != null)
          {
              LstDirectors.ItemsSource = data;
          }

          proxyClient.Close();
      }
```

Here, what I have done; I have changed the proxy implementation first, then I implemented the notification code, which will show every time that "**Directors Fetched**". Now, you might be thinking what exactly this instance context is. It is very simple to answer. Instance context is a wrapper for the implementer of the callback contract. Hence, it instantiated the instance of the instance context class and in the constructor sent the implementer of the callback contract, which is **this**. This is how the client gets the information about itself to the proxy. The proxy then use this information, stick in the header of the SOAP message, pass in to the service and

Pragmatic WCF

service gets to appoint an operation where it is looking for a callback channel, it knows how to create the one. With the above change in place, when I run the same, client window will stuck because of threading issue. Here, we got thread deadlock.

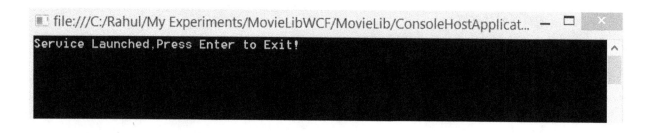

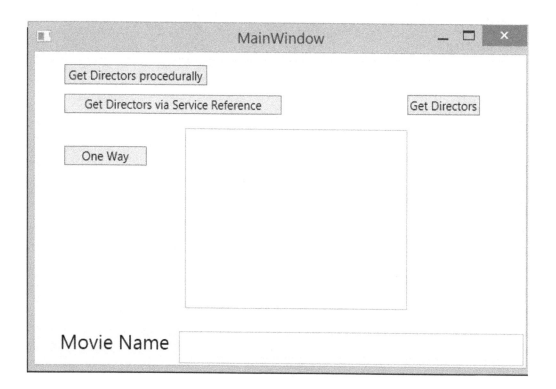

CLEARING DEADLOCK:-

Deadlock situation after default timeout will eventually go off, but let us discuss why this is happening. Callback is entering the client in UI thread; and UI happens to be busy now, it is in middle of something. Moreover, that something is not getting done here. Now, if you remember from previous threading chapter, we ran in the similar problem. And that time we

Pragmatic WCF

used synchronization context to fix the problem. Here, in the client, we cannot use service behavior, but we can use another behavior called callback behavior as shown below in the snippet.

```csharp
using System;
using System.Collections;
using System.Collections.Generic;
using System.ServiceModel;
using System.ServiceModel.Channels;
using System.Threading;
using System.Threading.Tasks;
using System.Windows;
using MovieLib.Client.Contracts;
using MovieLib.Client.ServiceReference1;
using MovieLib.Contracts;
using MovieLib.Proxies;

namespace MovieLib.Client
{
    /// <summary>
    /// Interaction logic for MainWindow.xaml
    /// </summary>

    [CallbackBehavior(UseSynchronizationContext = false)]
    public partial class MainWindow : Window, IUpdateMovieCallback
    {
        private MovieClient proxyClient = null;
        private SynchronizationContext synchronizationContext = null;
        public MainWindow()
        {
            InitializeComponent();
//          proxyClient = new MovieClient("1stEP");
           // proxyClient.Open();
           // synchronizationContext = SynchronizationContext.Current;
        }
```

Pragmatic WCF

```csharp
private async void Button_Click(object sender, RoutedEventArgs e)
{
    // MovieClient proxyClient = new MovieClient("1stEP");


    try
    {
        await Task.Run(() =>
        {
            IEnumerable<MovieData> data = proxyClient.GetDirectorNames();
            if (data != null)
            {
                SendOrPostCallback callback = (arg =>
                {
                    LstDirectors.ItemsSource = data;
                });
                synchronizationContext.Send(callback, true);
            }


            //   proxyClient.Close();
        });


    }
    catch (FaultException<ExceptionDetail> ex)
    {
        MessageBox.Show("Exception thrown by service.\n\r Exception Type:-" + ex +

            "Message:-" + ex.Detail.Message + "\n\r" +
            "Proxy State:- " + proxyClient.State);
    }


    catch (FaultException<ApplicationException> ex)
    {
        MessageBox.Show("Exception thrown by
FaultException<ApplicationException>.\n\r Exception Type:-" + ex +
```

Pragmatic WCF

```
                    "Message:-" + ex.Detail.Message + "\n\r" +

                    "Proxy State:- " + proxyClient.State);

        }


        catch (FaultException<DataNotFound> ex)

        {
            MessageBox.Show("Exception thrown by FaultException<DataNotFound>.\n\r
Exception Type:-" + ex +

                    "Message:-" + ex.Detail.Message + "\n\r" +

                    "User:- " + ex.Detail.User + "\n\r" +

                    "When:- " + ex.Detail.When + "\n\r" +

                    "Proxy State:- " + proxyClient.State);

        }


        catch (FaultException ex)

        {
            MessageBox.Show("Fault Exception thrown by service.\n\r Exception Type:-"
+ ex +

                    "Message:-" + ex.Message + "\n\r" +

                    "Proxy State:- " + proxyClient.State);

        }
        catch (Exception ex)

        {
            MessageBox.Show("Exception thrown by service.\n\r Exception Type:-" + ex+

                    ex.GetType().Name+"\n\r"+

                    "Message:-" + ex.Message + "\n\r"+

                    "Proxy State:- " + proxyClient.State);

        }
    }


    public void movieCallback()
    {
        MessageBox.Show("Directors Fetched");
    }
    private void Button_Click_1(object sender, RoutedEventArgs e)
    {
```

Pragmatic WCF

```
        EndpointAddress address = new
EndpointAddress("net.tcp://localhost:8010/MovieService");
        Binding binding = new NetTcpBinding();


        MovieClient proxyClient = new MovieClient(new
InstanceContext(this),binding,address);
        //MovieClient proxyClient = new MovieClient(binding, address);


        IEnumerable<MovieData> data = proxyClient.GetDirectorNames();


        if (data != null)
        {
            LstDirectors.ItemsSource = data;
        }


        proxyClient.Close();
    }


    private void btnInvoke_Click(object sender, RoutedEventArgs e)
    {
        EndpointAddress address = new
EndpointAddress("net.tcp://localhost:8011/MovieName");
        Binding binding = new NetTcpBinding();


        ChannelFactory<IMovieName> factory = new ChannelFactory<IMovieName>(binding,
address);


        //ChannelFactory<IMovieName> factory = new ChannelFactory<IMovieName>("");


        IMovieName proxy = factory.CreateChannel();


        string value = txtMovieName.Text;
        proxy.ShowMovie(value);


        factory.Close();
    }
```

Pragmatic WCF

```
        private void Button_Click_2(object sender, RoutedEventArgs e)
        {
            MovieServiceClient proxy = new MovieServiceClient();


            IEnumerable<MovieData> datas = proxy.GetDirectorNames();


            if (datas != null)
            {
                LstDirectors.ItemsSource = datas;
            }


            proxy.Close();


        }


        private void Button_Click_3(object sender, RoutedEventArgs e)
        {
            MovieClient proxy = new MovieClient("1stEP");
            proxy.OneWayOperation();
            MessageBox.Show("Hello From client");
            proxy.Close();
            MessageBox.Show("Proxy closed");
        }




    }
}
```

With the above change in place, when I go ahead and build the app, it will run fine and produce me the expected output. Here, I clicked the button **Get Directors Procedurally**.

Pragmatic WCF

Now, Directors Fetched will keep on coming until loop overs. In the end when you click on the counter button, it will list all the directors as shown below in the screen shot.

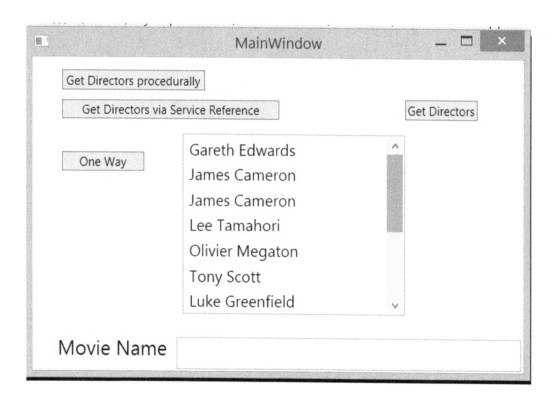

REPLACING MESSAGE-BOX:-

However, message box is not the correct way of handling threading issue, as this will not encounter the same. Now, instead of showing callback message via message-box, I will

Pragmatic WCF

accommodate the same via text-box. Therefore, in textbox I will simply print the message that Director Fetched. In order to achieve the same I have done the following change in my code. I have also added one additional textbox.

```
public void movieCallback()
    {
        // MessageBox.Show("Directors Fetched");
        directorFetched.Text = "Director Fetched";
    }
```

With the above change in place when I run the same, it will produce me the below error.

Pragmatic WCF

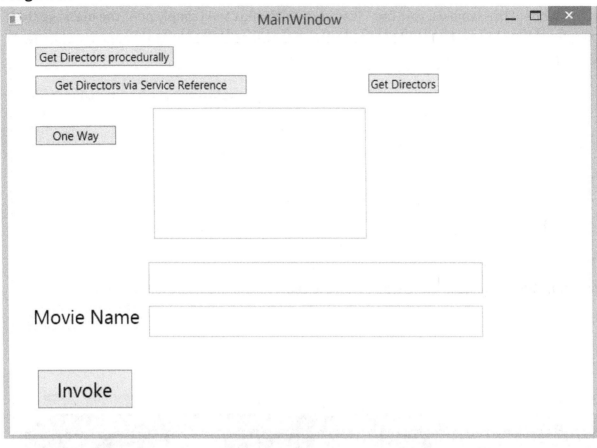

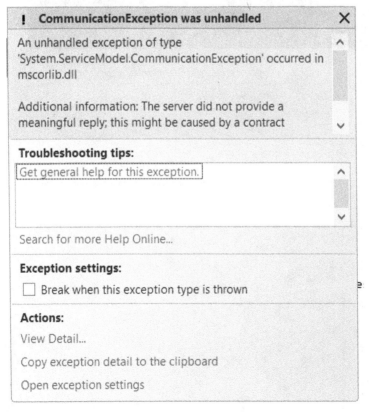

Pragmatic WCF

Now, this happened because I am in background thread and I cannot update the UI. Therefore, I have to marshal up. Hence, I need to use the old trick of synchronization context.

```
[CallbackBehavior(UseSynchronizationContext = false)]
    public partial class MainWindow : Window, IUpdateMovieCallback
    {
        private MovieClient proxyClient = null;
        private SynchronizationContext synchronizationContext = null;
        public MainWindow()
        {
            InitializeComponent();
            synchronizationContext = SynchronizationContext.Current;
        }
```

Now, I can use this to marshal the UI thread as shown below in the snippet.

```
public void movieCallback()
        {
            // MessageBox.Show("Directors Fetched");
            SendOrPostCallback sendOrPostCallback = new SendOrPostCallback(arg =>
            {
                directorFetched.Text =
                    "Director Fetched";
            });

            synchronizationContext.Send(sendOrPostCallback,null);
        }
```

With the above change in place, my exception will go, but when I invoke the operation, still UI is busy; it is not getting updated as shown below in the screen shot.

Pragmatic WCF

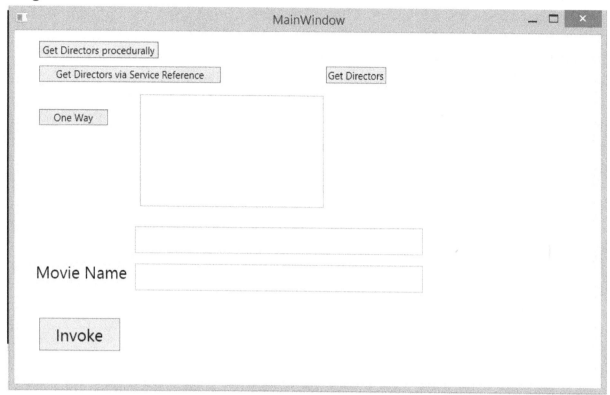

In order to fix the same, I need to keep my proxy code in the background thread and that will free up the UI. Now, when I do that I do not actually need the synchronization context and marshalling, but I always like the idea of freeing up the UI thread.

USING THREAD:-

In this case, I have changed the same to use thread. Below is the snippet for the same. Therefore, proxy code I have pushed on the worker thread so that UI thread remain free for update.

```
private void Button_Click_1(object sender, RoutedEventArgs e)
        {
            EndpointAddress address = new
EndpointAddress("net.tcp://localhost:8010/MovieService");
            Binding binding = new NetTcpBinding();
```

Pragmatic WCF

```csharp
        Thread thread = new Thread(() =>
        {
            MovieClient proxyClient = new MovieClient(new InstanceContext(this),
binding, address);

            IEnumerable<MovieData> data = proxyClient.GetDirectorNames();

            if (data != null)
            {
                LstDirectors.ItemsSource = data;
            }

            proxyClient.Close();
        });

        thread.Start();
    }
```

With the above change in place, when I run the same, it will produce me the desired output as shown below in the screen shot.

Pragmatic WCF

Obviously above example just to demonstrate the threading issue as using textbox is not the best fit here. Nevertheless, good enough to prove the point.

CHANGING THREAD TO TASK:-

To change this thread code to Task is actually quite easy. Using task-based programming is much better and safer than using thread programming. Below is the changed code for the same.

```
private async void Button_Click_1(object sender, RoutedEventArgs e)
    {
            EndpointAddress address = new
EndpointAddress("net.tcp://localhost:8010/MovieService");
            Binding binding = new NetTcpBinding();
```

Pragmatic WCF

```
await Task.Run(() =>
{
    MovieClient proxyClient = new MovieClient(new InstanceContext(this),
binding, address);
    //MovieClient proxyClient = new MovieClient(binding, address);

    IEnumerable<MovieData> data = proxyClient.GetDirectorNames();

    if (data != null)
    {
        LstDirectors.ItemsSource = data;
    }

    proxyClient.Close();
});

}
```

With the above change in place, it will work exactly same but in a much better fashion.

SUMMARY:-

In this section, we have seen different ways of handling Operations. We started with legacy and simpler pattern of request-response. Then, we tested the same with One-Way operation. Later on, we saw deadlock situations and solution for the same. We also saw how to handle callback and handle threading issues at the client level. Then, we saw more realistic situation by replacing message box with the embedded control on the UI itself. Last but not the least we saw how to use Task to handle the same situation.

Pragmatic WCF

CHAPTER 11: SECURITY

WHAT DO you find in this CHAPTER?

- Introduction
- Security Scenarios
- Authentication
- Authorization
- Running with No Security
- Running with Security
- Protection Levels
- Alternate Credentials
- Role-Based
- Intranet Web App
- Running Web Client
- Internet Web App
- Security Mode
- Setting Behavior
- Certificate Creation
- Configuring Certificate
- Client Configuration
- ASP.NET Providers
- Summary

INTRODUCTION:-

We have reached to the end of the course. Security is one of the most important aspects of any application. More secure you make your app; more reliable it will be. There are many details and lot of component involves in security; that is why I kept this chapter for last. Because, in this section, you need all the learnings what you have learnt so far. Let me put the topics upfront, which we will be discussing in detail.

Pragmatic WCF

- Security Modes
- Protection Levels
- Authentication
- Authorization
- Identities
- Certificates

SECURITY SCENARIOS:-

Here, I am trying to keep the things as much real as possible. What I am doing here; I am covering two most popular scenarios, one for intranet means for internal stuff and other for internet for outside world.

1. Intranet Scenario: - This scenario comes into picture when clients are inside Firewall. Hence, in this case TCP binding will be used. In addition, it is going to incorporate built in windows authentication/authorization. This one is easy to setup and very secure as well.

2. Internet Scenario: - This scenario is little bit complicated because this one is designed for the client, which sits outside the firewall. Here, it uses HTTP binding. We do not have built in security support as we have for TCP. Because, of this nature we need to bring certificates to provide authentication and authorization.

In order to cover these scenarios, we must know about identities first. **Identities** are the heart of .NET Security. This is something, which is going to come in both Internet and Intranet scenario and they will vary in each scenario. The main Identity, which I am discussing here, is, **Client Identity** also known as **Primary Identity**. Moreover, this client identity is going to pass in the service. Now, it is very important to understand that when I am saying client identity, I am referring to the caller of the WCF services. Now, let us see how to obtain the same:-

1. Token/Host Identity: - This one is obtainable from the **WindowsIdentity.GetCurrent()** static method. Now, this host identity is the identity that host the process means service host is running in it and this is the identity, which is used to access the resources by service.

2. Primary Identity: - Primary Identity is the identity of the client means the caller. This can be accessed using **ServicesSecurityContext.Current.PrimaryIdentity.**

Pragmatic WCF

3. Windows Identity: - This one is same as primary identity if windows authentication is used otherwise it will be null. This can be accessed using **ServicesSecurityContext.Current.WindowsIdentity.**

All the above listed identities are the implementation of **IIdentity** Interface.

AUTHENTICATION:-

In this section, we will start with windows authentication, which we will have WCF client create a windows token for us and send the same to the service. WCF sends these credentials automatically through the proxy. We can alter these credentials, which we will see in a moment. As I said, client credentials sent to the service as a token which means they are received as a primary identity. If you are dealing with windows app, then client will be Windows User (My Credentials) in this case. However, if you are dealing with web interface like an ASP.NET application, in that case client will be IIS.

AUTHORIZATION:-

Once the caller is authenticated, they have to be authorized to use the operation that they requested. Now, authorization is performed against the primary identity, identity of the caller. Therefore, once the service constructor is hit, WCF creates Windows Principle and wraps primary identity and associated groups. This principle is placed under the **Thread.CurrentPrinciple** property. Every principle in .NET security system is the implementation of **IPrinciple** Interface. To authorize permission, we can do couple of things here. However, the easiest way of doing this is using **PrinciplePermission** attribute on roles. Here, you can demand authorization based on specific roles or user name. Internally, this demand checks for the role using **Thread.Current.IsInRole.**

RUNNING WITH NO SECURITY:-

In this section, we will start with few changes in code. I will revert all the changes what I have done in operation's chapter and then start implementing security pieces here. Therefore, the first thing, which I am going to do, is actually turn on the security. Below in the app.config of console host, I have introduced the same. However, by default in TCP binding security is turned on. Hence, I will begin by turning off the security.

Pragmatic WCF

```xml
<bindings>
  <netTcpBinding>
    <binding name="tcpSecurity">
      <security mode="">
    </binding>
  </netTcpBinding>
</bindings>
<behaviors>
  <serviceBehaviors>
    <behavior>
      <serviceDebug includeExceptionDetailInFaults="true"/>
    </behavior>
  </serviceBehaviors>
```

📄	None
📄	Transport
📄	Message
📄	TransportWithMessageCredential

As you can see in the above screen shot, you will get complete intellisense support from Visual Studio while setting the stuffs explicitly. Since, these are binding settings, hence these needs to be set on the both sides of the wire. Below are the configs for server side and client side.

```xml
<?xml version="1.0" encoding="utf-8"?>

<configuration>

  <configSections>

    <!-- For more information on Entity Framework configuration, visit
http://go.microsoft.com/fwlink/?LinkID=237468 -->

    <section name="entityFramework"
type="System.Data.Entity.Internal.ConfigFile.EntityFrameworkSection, EntityFramework,
Version=6.0.0.0, Culture=neutral, PublicKeyToken=b77a5c561934e089"
requirePermission="false" />

  </configSections>

  <startup>

    <supportedRuntime version="v4.0" sku=".NETFramework,Version=v4.5" />

  </startup>

  <entityFramework>

    <defaultConnectionFactory
type="System.Data.Entity.Infrastructure.SqlConnectionFactory, EntityFramework" />

    <providers>

      <provider invariantName="System.Data.SqlClient"
type="System.Data.Entity.SqlServer.SqlProviderServices, EntityFramework.SqlServer" />

    </providers>

  </entityFramework>
```

Pragmatic WCF

```xml
  <connectionStrings>

    <add name="MoviesReviewProd" connectionString="Data
Source=8133GTVZ1\SQLEXPRESS;Initial Catalog=MoviesReviewProd;Integrated Security=True"
providerName="System.Data.SqlClient" />

  </connectionStrings>

 <system.serviceModel>

  <services>

    <service name="MovieLib.Services.MovieManager">


      <endpoint address="net.tcp://localhost:8010/MovieService"
                binding="netTcpBinding"
                contract="MovieLib.Contracts.IMovieService"
bindingConfiguration="tcpSecurity"/>

      <endpoint address="http://localhost/MovieService"
                binding="basicHttpBinding"
                contract="MovieLib.Contracts.IMovieService"/>

    </service>

  </services>

  <bindings>

    <netTcpBinding>

      <binding name="tcpSecurity">

        <security mode="None"/>

      </binding>

    </netTcpBinding>

  </bindings>

  <behaviors>

    <serviceBehaviors>

      <behavior>

        <serviceDebug includeExceptionDetailInFaults="true"/>

      </behavior>

    </serviceBehaviors>

  </behaviors>

 </system.serviceModel>

</configuration>
```

Pragmatic WCF

Client Side:-

```xml
<?xml version="1.0" encoding="utf-8" ?>
<configuration>
  <startup>
    <supportedRuntime version="v4.0" sku=".NETFramework,Version=v4.5" />
  </startup>
  <system.serviceModel>
    <bindings>
      <basicHttpBinding>
        <binding name="BasicHttpBinding_IMovieService" />
      </basicHttpBinding>
      <netTcpBinding>
        <binding name="tcpSecurity">
          <security mode="None"/>
        </binding>
      </netTcpBinding>
    </bindings>
    <client>
      <endpoint address="net.tcp://localhost:8010/MovieService" binding="netTcpBinding"
        contract="MovieLib.Contracts.IMovieService" name="1stEP"
bindingConfiguration="tcpSecurity" />
      <endpoint address="http://localhost/MovieService" binding="basicHttpBinding"
        contract="MovieLib.Contracts.IMovieService" name="2ndEP" />
      <endpoint address="net.tcp://localhost:8011/MovieName" binding="netTcpBinding"
        contract="MovieLib.Client.Contracts.IMovieName" />
    </client>
  </system.serviceModel>
</configuration>
```

Now, let us go ahead and set the identity in the file. Therefore, if you recall we have talked about Host Identity, Primary Identity and Windows Identity. As you can see below in the screen shot, windows identity is part of Security features as highlighted by visual studio.

Pragmatic WCF

```
string windowsIdentity = windowsi
```
```
    WindowsIdentity (in System.Security.Principal)
    WindowsImpersonationContext (in System.Security.Principal)
```
```
try
{
```

Now, the last one is Thread identity and this one comes from thread current principle. Below, I have pasted my modified Movie Manager code.

```csharp
using System;
using System.Collections.Generic;
using System.Linq;
using System.Security.Principal;
using System.ServiceModel;
using System.Threading;
using System.Windows.Forms;
using MovieLib.Contracts;
using MovieLib.Data.Entities;
using MovieLib.Data.Repositories;
using MovieLib.Data.Repository_Interfaces;

namespace MovieLib.Services
{
    [ServiceBehavior(InstanceContextMode = InstanceContextMode.Single,
        ConcurrencyMode = ConcurrencyMode.Multiple,
        IncludeExceptionDetailInFaults = true)]
    public class MovieManager : IMovieService
    {
        private IMovieRepository _iMovieRepository;
        private int _counter = 0;
        public MovieManager()
        {


        }
```

Pragmatic WCF

```csharp
public MovieManager(IMovieRepository iMovieRepository)
{

    _iMovieRepository = iMovieRepository;

}
public IEnumerable<MovieData> GetDirectorNames()
{

    string hostIdentity = WindowsIdentity.GetCurrent().Name;
    string primaryIdentity = ServiceSecurityContext.Current.PrimaryIdentity.Name;
    string windowsIdentity = ServiceSecurityContext.Current.WindowsIdentity.Name;
    string threadIdentity = Thread.CurrentPrincipal.Identity.Name;


    List<MovieData> movieData = new List<MovieData>();


        IMovieRepository movieRepository = _iMovieRepository ?? new
MovieRepository();


        IEnumerable<Movie> movies = movieRepository.GetMovies();


    if (movies.Count() != 0)
    {
        foreach (Movie movie in movies)
        {
            movieData.Add(new MovieData()
            {
                DirectorName = movie.DirectorName
            });
        }
    }
    else
    {
        //throw new Exception("List is empty");
        // throw new FaultException("List is empty");
        //ApplicationException ex = new ApplicationException("List is empty");
```

Pragmatic WCF

```
                 //throw new FaultException<ApplicationException>(ex,"Wrong DB instance");


          DataNotFound ex = new DataNotFound()
          {
              Message = "Data Not Found",
              When = DateTime.Now.ToString(),
              User = "Rahul"
          };
          throw new FaultException<DataNotFound>(ex,"Custom Exception");
      }

      _counter++;
      //Console.WriteLine("Counter:- {0}",_counter);
      MessageBox.Show("Counter:-" +_counter);




      return movieData;
  }




  void IMovieService.UpdateMovieDirector(string moviename, string director)
  {
      throw new NotImplementedException();
  }
  }
}
```

After the constructor of the service is hit, primary identity is placed in thread identity. During the constructor invocation of the service Thread, identity will be null but Primary identity will be there. Now, let us run the code and show you the value by putting break point there. One point to note here, when security is off, only host identity will be obtainable. Other identities will remain null as shown below in the screen shot.

Pragmatic WCF

```csharp
public IEnumerable<MovieData> GetDirectorNames()
{

    string hostIdentity = WindowsIdentity.GetCurrent().Name;
    string primaryI[ ● hostIdentity  Q ▼ "AMERICAS\\Rahul_Sahay"  ▭ ]t.PrimaryIdentity.Name;
    string windowsIdentity = ServiceSecurityContext.Current.WindowsIdentity.Name;
    string threadIdentity = Thread.CurrentPrincipal.Identity.Name;
```

RUNNING WITH SECURITY:-

Let us go ahead and enable the security. Let us set the same to Transport Mode. Therefore, I can set the mode to Transport, Message or both.

```xml
<bindings>
  <netTcpBinding>
    <binding name="tcpSecurity">
      <security mode=""/>
    </binding>
  </netTcpBinding>
</bindings>
<!--<behaviors>
  <serviceBehaviors>
```

📄 None
📄 Transport
📄 Message
📄 TransportWithMessageCredential

Once, I set the mode to Transport. I will get the access to inner node as shown below.

```xml
<bindings>
  <netTcpBinding>
    <binding name="tcpSecurity">
      <security mode="Transport">
        |
      </
    </bi
  </netT
</bindin
```

🔲	<!--
🔲	<?
🔲	<message
🔲	<transport

Pragmatic WCF

Now, the property, which I am looking here, is **ClientCredentialType.** We will come to
ProtectionLevel property at later point of time.

```
<!--<endpoint address="MEX"
          binding    clientCredentialType
          contrac    lockAllAttributesExcept    -->
</service>                lockAllElementsExcept
</services>               lockAttributes
<bindings>                lockElements
  <netTcpBinding>         lockItem
    <binding name="      protectionLevel
      <security mod
        <transport
      </security>
    </binding>
  </netTcpBinding>
</bindings>
```

```
<bindings>
  <netTcpBinding>                      None
    <binding name="tcpSecurity">       Windows
      <security mode="Transport">      Certificate
        <transport clientCredentialType=""
      </security>
    </binding>
  </netTcpBinding>
</bindings>
```

Therefore, the **ClientCredentialType** is going to determine what the client uses to send to the
service as its credentials and because we are using windows authentication, hence we will use
Windows. This will tell use the windows token to authenticate at the service side. Once I am
done with binding changes, I need to duplicate the same on the client side as well as shown
below.

```
<bindings>
  <netTcpBinding>
    <binding name="tcpSecurity">
      <security mode="Transport">
```

Pragmatic WCF

```
        <transport clientCredentialType="Windows"></transport>

    </security>

  </binding>

 </netTcpBinding>

</bindings>
```

Now, let us go ahead and test the app again. In this case, it will have all the four identities but with the same value as I am running windows app, hence it is using my identity at all the places.

```
public IEnumerable<MovieData> GetDirectorNames()
{
    string hostIdentity = WindowsIdentity.GetCurrent().Name;
    string primaryI[● hostIdentity  🔍 ▾ "AMERICAS\\Rahul_Sahay" ▭]t.PrimaryIdentity.Name;
    string windowsIdentity = ServiceSecurityContext.Current.WindowsIdentity.Name;
    string threadIdentity = Thread.CurrentPrincipal.Identity.Name;
```

```
    string hostIdentity = WindowsIdentity.GetCurrent().Name;
    string primaryIdentity = ServiceSecurityContext.Current.PrimaryIdentity.Name;
    string windowsI[● primaryIdentity  🔍 ▾ "AMERICAS\\Rahul_Sahay" ▭]WindowsIdentity.Name;
    string threadIdentity = Thread.CurrentPrincipal.Identity.Name;
```

```
    string hostIdentity = WindowsIdentity.GetCurrent().Name;
    string primaryIdentity = ServiceSecurityContext.Current.PrimaryIdentity.Name;
    string windowsIdentity = ServiceSecurityContext.Current.WindowsIdentity.Name;
    string threadIdentity[● windowsIdentity  🔍 ▾ "AMERICAS\\Rahul_Sahay" ▭]
```

```
    string hostIdentity = WindowsIdentity.GetCurrent().Name;
    string primaryIdentity = ServiceSecurityContext.Current.PrimaryIdentity.Name;
    string windowsIdentity = ServiceSecurityContext.Current.WindowsIdentity.Name;
    string threadIdentity = Thread.CurrentPrincipal.Identity.Name;
            [● threadIdentity  🔍 ▾ "AMERICAS\\Rahul_Sahay" ▭]
    List<MovieData> movieData = new List<MovieData>();
```

Pragmatic WCF

PROTECTION LEVELS:-

Let us talk about protection level here. Default value of protection level is **EncryptAndSign**. However, let me set the same to sign and duplicate the same in client section as well.

```xml
<bindings>
  <netTcpBinding>
    <binding name="tcpSecurity">
      <security mode="Transport">
        <transport clientCredentialType="Windows" pr/>
      </security>
    </binding>
  </netTcpBinding>
</bindings>
<!--<behaviors>
  <serviceBehaviors>
    <behavior>
      <serviceMetadata httpGetEnabled="true"/>
    </behavior>
  </serviceBehaviors>
</behaviors>-->
```

```
🔧 lockAllAttributesExcept
🔧 lockAllElementsExcept
🔧 lockAttributes
🔧 lockElements
🔧 lockItem
🔧 protectionLevel
```

```xml
<bindings>

    <netTcpBinding>

        <binding name="tcpSecurity">

          <security mode="Transport">

            <transport clientCredentialType="Windows" protectionLevel="Sign"/>

          </security>

        </binding>

    </netTcpBinding>

  </bindings>
```

Once, I set the same at both the places. Then, I can go ahead in my contracts section and add protection level at the operation contract level or service contract level. What it tells here is define the minimum; hence, I can go ahead and define like this.

```csharp
using System;
using System.Collections.Generic;
using System.Net.Security;
```

Pragmatic WCF

```csharp
using System.ServiceModel;


namespace MovieLib.Contracts
{
    [ServiceContract(ProtectionLevel = ProtectionLevel.EncryptAndSign)]
    public interface IMovieService
    {
        [OperationContract]
        [FaultContract(typeof(ApplicationException))]
        [FaultContract(typeof(DataNotFound))]
        IEnumerable<MovieData> GetDirectorNames();


        [OperationContract]
        [TransactionFlow(TransactionFlowOption.Allowed)]
        void UpdateMovieDirector(string moviename, string director);
    }
}
```

With the current configuration, my service contract is demanding full protection level but binding is configured with minimum protection. Hence, this will blow up.

Pragmatic WCF

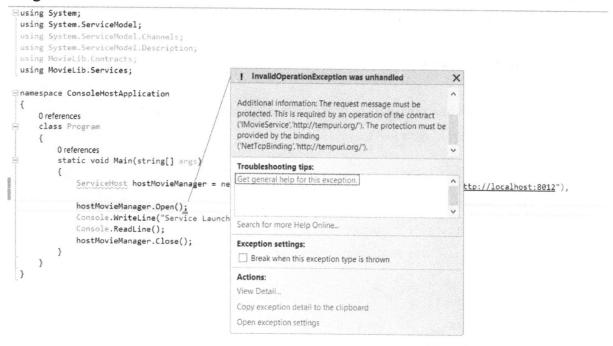

```
using System;
using System.ServiceModel;
using System.ServiceModel.Channels;
using System.ServiceModel.Description;
using MovieLib.Contracts;
using MovieLib.Services;

namespace ConsoleHostApplication
{
    0 references
    class Program
    {
        0 references
        static void Main(string[] args)
        {
            ServiceHost hostMovieManager = ne                              ttp://localhost:8012"),

            hostMovieManager.Open();
            Console.WriteLine("Service Launch
            Console.ReadLine();
            hostMovieManager.Close();
        }
    }
}
```

InvalidOperationException was unhandled ✕

Additional information: The request message must be protected. This is required by an operation of the contract ('IMovieService','http://tempuri.org/'). The protection must be provided by the binding ('NetTcpBinding','http://tempuri.org/').

Troubleshooting tips:

Get general help for this exception.

Search for more Help Online...

Exception settings:

☐ Break when this exception type is thrown

Actions:

View Detail...

Copy exception detail to the clipboard

Open exception settings

Therefore, this is how you can enforce a specific protection level.

ALTERNATE CREDENTIALS:-

You can set alternate credentials in the client at proxy level as shown below in the snippet. Here, I would like to show how to send alternate credentials to the proxy.

```
private async void Button_Click(object sender, RoutedEventArgs e)
    {
        // MovieClient proxyClient = new MovieClient("1stEP");


        proxyClient.ClientCredentials.Windows.ClientCredential.Domain = "Americas";
        proxyClient.ClientCredentials.Windows.ClientCredential.UserName =
"WCFClient";

        proxyClient.ClientCredentials.Windows.ClientCredential.Password =
"WCFPassword";


        try
        {
            await Task.Run(() =>
```

Pragmatic WCF

```
                {
                    IEnumerable<MovieData> data = proxyClient.GetDirectorNames();

                    if (data != null)
                    {
                        SendOrPostCallback callback = (arg =>
                        {
                            LstDirectors.ItemsSource = data;
                        });
                        synchronizationContext.Send(callback, true);
                    }


                    //    proxyClient.Close();
                });


            }
            catch (FaultException<ExceptionDetail> ex)
            {
                MessageBox.Show("Exception thrown by service.\n\r Exception Type:-" + ex
+
                    "Message:-" + ex.Detail.Message + "\n\r" +
                    "Proxy State:- " + proxyClient.State);
            }


            catch (FaultException<ApplicationException> ex)
            {
                MessageBox.Show("Exception thrown by
FaultException<ApplicationException>.\n\r Exception Type:-" + ex +
                    "Message:-" + ex.Detail.Message + "\n\r" +
                    "Proxy State:- " + proxyClient.State);
            }


            catch (FaultException<DataNotFound> ex)
            {
                MessageBox.Show("Exception thrown by FaultException<DataNotFound>.\n\r
Exception Type:-" + ex +
                    "Message:-" + ex.Detail.Message + "\n\r" +
                    "User:- " + ex.Detail.User + "\n\r" +
```

Pragmatic WCF

```
            "When:- " + ex.Detail.When + "\n\r" +

            "Proxy State:- " + proxyClient.State);

    }


    catch (FaultException ex)

    {

        MessageBox.Show("Fault Exception thrown by service.\n\r Exception Type:-"
+ ex +

            "Message:-" + ex.Message + "\n\r" +

            "Proxy State:- " + proxyClient.State);

    }

    catch (Exception ex)

    {

        MessageBox.Show("Exception thrown by service.\n\r Exception Type:-" + ex+

            ex.GetType().Name+"\n\r"+

            "Message:-" + ex.Message + "\n\r"+

            "Proxy State:- " + proxyClient.State);

    }

}
```

With the above change in place, when I run the app, then you will see the difference in primary
identity as caller identity changed to the alternate credential. In addition, before doing the
same you need to create one new user in your system with above credentials. Then, windows
and thread identity will also show new identity.

ROLE-BASED:-

You can also go ahead and secure your service by including role-based authentication like
shown below

Pragmatic WCF

```
1 reference
public MovieManager(IMovieRepository iMovieRepository)
{
    _iMovieRepositor (SecurityAction action, [SecurityAction Action], [bool Authenticated], [string Name], [string Role], [bool Unrestricted])
}                     Initializes a new instance of the PrincipalPermissionAttribute class with the specified SecurityAction.
                      action: One of the SecurityAction values.
[PrincipalPermission(sec)]
7 references
public IEnumerable    🔲 SecurityAction
{                     🔲 SecurityAttribute
                      🔲 SecurityIDType
    string hostIde    🔲 SecurityIdentifier        t().Name;
    string primary    🔲 SecurityMode              .Current.PrimaryIdentity.Name;
    string windows    🔲 SecurityPermission        .Current.WindowsIdentity.Name;
    string threadI    🔲 SecurityPermissionAttribute   .Identity.Name;
                      🔲 SecurityPermissionFlag
    List<MovieData    🔲 SecurityAction.Assert     ();
                      🔲 SecurityAction.Demand
                      🔲 SecurityAction.Deny
    IMovieRepository movieRepository = _iMovieRepository ?? new MovieRepository();

    IEnumerable<Movie> movies = movieRepository.GetMovies();
```

```csharp
[PrincipalPermission(SecurityAction.Demand, Role = "Administrators")]
    public IEnumerable<MovieData> GetDirectorNames()
    {

        string hostIdentity = WindowsIdentity.GetCurrent().Name;

        string primaryIdentity = ServiceSecurityContext.Current.PrimaryIdentity.Name;

        string windowsIdentity = ServiceSecurityContext.Current.WindowsIdentity.Name;

        string threadIdentity = Thread.CurrentPrincipal.Identity.Name;


        List<MovieData> movieData = new List<MovieData>();



            IMovieRepository movieRepository = _iMovieRepository ?? new
MovieRepository();


            IEnumerable<Movie> movies = movieRepository.GetMovies();


        if (movies.Count() != 0)
        {
        foreach (Movie movie in movies)
        {
            movieData.Add(new MovieData()
```

Pragmatic WCF

```
            {
                    DirectorName = movie.DirectorName
            });
        }
    }
    else
    {

        DataNotFound ex = new DataNotFound()
        {
            Message = "Data Not Found",
            When = DateTime.Now.ToString(),
            User = "Rahul"
        };
        throw new FaultException<DataNotFound>(ex,"Custom Exception");
    }

    _counter++;
    //Console.WriteLine("Counter:- {0}",_counter);
    MessageBox.Show("Counter:-" +_counter);



        return movieData;
    }
```

With this change in place, when you try to run your app with alternate credential, it will blow up.

Pragmatic WCF

Exception thrown by service.
Exception Type:-System.ServiceModel.Security.SecurityAccessDeniedException: Access is denied.

Server stack trace:
  at System.ServiceModel.Channels.ServiceChannel.ThrowIfFaultUnderstood(Message reply, MessageFault fault, String action, MessageVersion version, FaultConverter faultConverter)
  at System.ServiceModel.Channels.ServiceChannel.HandleReply(ProxyOperationRuntime operation, ProxyRpc& rpc)
  at System.ServiceModel.Channels.ServiceChannel.Call(String action, Boolean oneway, ProxyOperationRuntime operation, Object[] ins, Object[] outs, TimeSpan timeout)
  at System.ServiceModel.Channels.ServiceChannelProxy.InvokeService(IMethodCallMessage methodCall, ProxyOperationRuntime operation)
  at System.ServiceModel.Channels.ServiceChannelProxy.Invoke(IMessage message)

Exception rethrown at [0]:
  at System.Runtime.Remoting.Proxies.RealProxy.HandleReturnMessage(IMessage reqMsg, IMessage retMsg)
  at System.Runtime.Remoting.Proxies.RealProxy.PrivateInvoke(MessageData& msgData, Int32 type)
  at MovieLib.Contracts.IMovieService.GetDirectorNames()
  at MovieLib.Proxies.MovieClient.GetDirectorNames() in c:\Rahul\Books\WCF\backup\20th May - Copy\MovieLib\MovieLib.Proxies\MovieClient.cs:line 22
  at MovieLib.Client.MainWindow.<Button_Click>b__0() in c:\Rahul\Books\WCF\backup\20th May - Copy\MovieLib\MovieLib.Client\MainWindow.xaml.cs:line 44
  at System.Threading.Tasks.Task.InnerInvoke()
  at System.Threading.Tasks.Task.Execute()
--- End of stack trace from previous location where exception was thrown ---
  at System.Runtime.CompilerServices.TaskAwaiter.ThrowForNonSuccess(Task task)
  at System.Runtime.CompilerServices.TaskAwaiter.HandleNonSuccessAndDebuggerNotification(Task task)
  at System.Runtime.CompilerServices.TaskAwaiter.GetResult()
  at MovieLib.Client.MainWindow.<Button_Click>d__6.MoveNext() in c:\Rahul\Books\WCF\backup\20th May - Copy\MovieLib\MovieLib.Client\MainWindow.xaml.cs:line
42SecurityAccessDeniedException
Message:-Access is denied.
Proxy State:- Opened

OK

However, if I just remove the alternate credentials from client, then it will function as normal as expected.

Pragmatic WCF

INTRANET WEB APP:-

The examples you have seen for has been from my desktop app. Remember the user in the desktop application, the client is me (**Rahul_Sahay**) in this context. In the case of intranet web application or browser-based application inside the firewall, client credentials are different. These client credentials are those of IIS. Now, the code itself makes the proxy call and perform soft-impersonation just before the service call. This allows the browser client temporarily super imposed as the caller. In order to create this scenario, I am going to create new project for the web client as shown below in the screen shot.

Pragmatic WCF

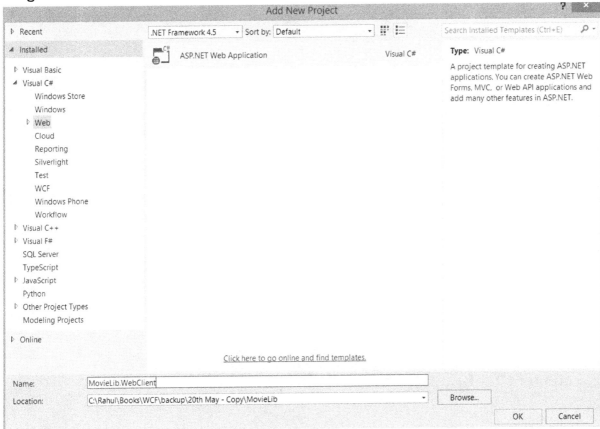

Pragmatic WCF

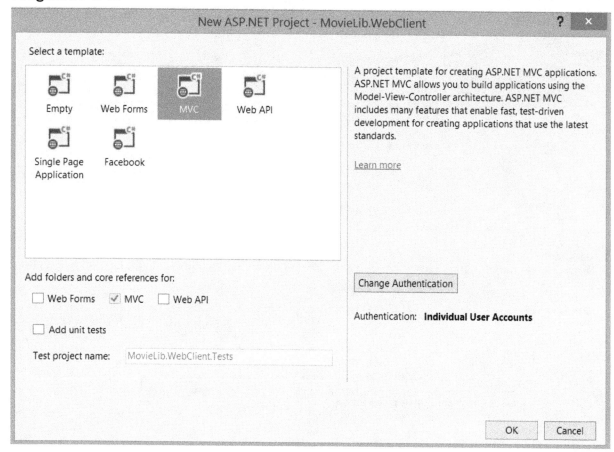

Once, the project got created successfully, it will look like

Pragmatic WCF

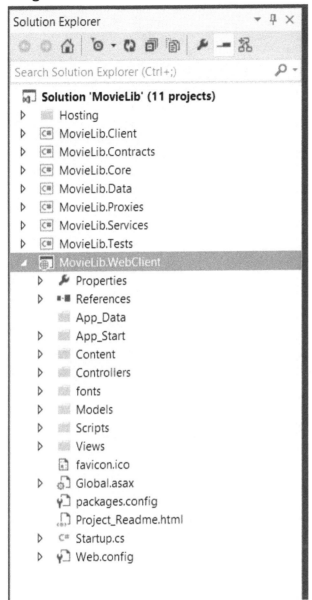

Now this solution has really become huge, now it is a collection of 11 projects. Anyways, let us go and setup the client configuration in the web.config file as shown below.

```
<?xml version="1.0" encoding="utf-8"?>
<!--
  For more information on how to configure your ASP.NET application, please visit
  http://go.microsoft.com/fwlink/?LinkId=301880
```

Pragmatic WCF

```xml
    -->
<configuration>
  <configSections>
    <!-- For more information on Entity Framework configuration, visit
http://go.microsoft.com/fwlink/?LinkID=237468 -->
    <section name="entityFramework"
type="System.Data.Entity.Internal.ConfigFile.EntityFrameworkSection, EntityFramework,
Version=6.0.0.0, Culture=neutral, PublicKeyToken=b77a5c561934e089"
requirePermission="false" />
  </configSections>
  <connectionStrings>
    <add name="MoviesReviewProd" connectionString="Data
Source=8133GTVZ1\SQLEXPRESS;Initial Catalog=MoviesReviewProd;Integrated Security=True"
providerName="System.Data.SqlClient" />
  </connectionStrings>
  <appSettings>
    <add key="webpages:Version" value="3.0.0.0" />
    <add key="webpages:Enabled" value="false" />
    <add key="ClientValidationEnabled" value="true" />
    <add key="UnobtrusiveJavaScriptEnabled" value="true" />
  </appSettings>
  <system.web>
<authentication mode="Windows" />
    <compilation debug="true" targetFramework="4.5" />
    <httpRuntime targetFramework="4.5" />
  </system.web>
  <system.webServer>
    <modules>
      <remove name="FormsAuthenticationModule" />
    </modules>
  </system.webServer>
  <system.serviceModel>
    <bindings>
      <basicHttpBinding>
        <binding name="BasicHttpBinding_IMovieService" />
      </basicHttpBinding>
      <netTcpBinding>
```

Pragmatic WCF

```
            <binding name="tcpSecurity" >

              <security mode="Transport">

                <transport clientCredentialType="Windows" protectionLevel="Sign"/>

              </security>

            </binding>

          </netTcpBinding>

        </bindings>

        <client>

          <endpoint address="net.tcp://localhost:8010/MovieService" binding="netTcpBinding"

            contract="MovieLib.Contracts.IMovieService" name="1stEP"
bindingConfiguration="tcpSecurity" />

          <endpoint address="http://localhost/MovieService" binding="basicHttpBinding"

            contract="MovieLib.Contracts.IMovieService" name="2ndEP" />

          <endpoint address="net.tcp://localhost:8011/MovieName" binding="netTcpBinding"

            contract="MovieLib.Client.Contracts.IMovieName" />

        </client>

      </system.serviceModel>

      <runtime>

        <assemblyBinding xmlns="urn:schemas-microsoft-com:asm.v1">

          <dependentAssembly>

            <assemblyIdentity name="System.Web.Helpers" publicKeyToken="31bf3856ad364e35" />

            <bindingRedirect oldVersion="1.0.0.0-3.0.0.0" newVersion="3.0.0.0" />

          </dependentAssembly>

          <dependentAssembly>

            <assemblyIdentity name="System.Web.Mvc" publicKeyToken="31bf3856ad364e35" />

            <bindingRedirect oldVersion="1.0.0.0-5.0.0.0" newVersion="5.0.0.0" />

          </dependentAssembly>

          <dependentAssembly>

            <assemblyIdentity name="System.Web.WebPages" publicKeyToken="31bf3856ad364e35" />

            <bindingRedirect oldVersion="1.0.0.0-3.0.0.0" newVersion="3.0.0.0" />

          </dependentAssembly>

          <dependentAssembly>

            <assemblyIdentity name="WebGrease" publicKeyToken="31bf3856ad364e35" />

            <bindingRedirect oldVersion="1.0.0.0-1.5.2.14234" newVersion="1.5.2.14234" />

          </dependentAssembly>

        </assemblyBinding>
```

Pragmatic WCF

```
  </runtime>

  <entityFramework>

    <defaultConnectionFactory
type="System.Data.Entity.Infrastructure.SqlConnectionFactory, EntityFramework" />

    <providers>

      <provider invariantName="System.Data.SqlClient"
type="System.Data.Entity.SqlServer.SqlProviderServices, EntityFramework.SqlServer" />

    </providers>

  </entityFramework>

</configuration>
```

Once, the configs change is done, let us change the project settings as shown below.

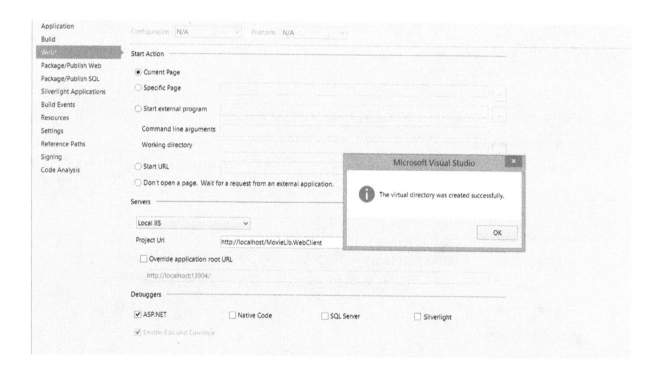

Also, below is my controller code for the same.

```
using System;
```

Pragmatic WCF

```csharp
using System.Collections.Generic;

using System.Linq;

using System.Web;

using System.Web.Mvc;

using MovieLib.Contracts;

using MovieLib.Proxies;


namespace MovieLib.WebClient.Controllers
{
    public class HomeController : Controller
    {
        public ActionResult Index()
        {
            return View();
        }


        public ActionResult About()
        {
            ViewBag.Message = "Your application description page.";


            return View();
        }


        public ActionResult Contact()
        {
            ViewBag.Message = "Your contact page.";


            return View();
        }


        private MovieClient proxyClient = null;
        public ActionResult MovieList()
        {
            proxyClient = new MovieClient("1stEP");
            proxyClient.Open();
            IEnumerable<MovieData> data = proxyClient.GetDirectorNames();
```

Pragmatic WCF

```
        proxyClient.Close();

        return View();

    }

  }

}
```

One more important setting I would like to show you is windows authentication, which I set in the web.config.

```
<authentication mode="Windows" />
```

Now, let us go ahead in the IIS Settings and set the same to Windows Authentication,

Authentication

Group by: No Grouping ▼

Name	Status	Response Type
Anonymous Authentication	Enabled	
ASP.NET Impersonation	Disabled	
Basic Authentication	Disabled	HTTP 401 Challenge
Digest Authentication	Disabled	HTTP 401 Challenge
Forms Authentication	Disabled	HTTP 302 Login/Redirect
Windows Authentication	Enabled	HTTP 401 Challenge

I also want to show you Site's basic setting which says currently I am running as Pass-Through connection.

Pragmatic WCF

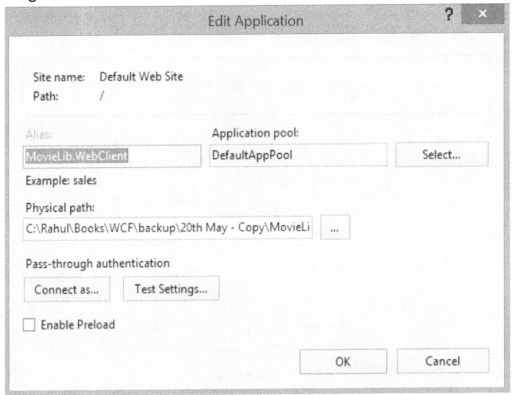

Now, when I run the app from browser, it will produce me the below output.

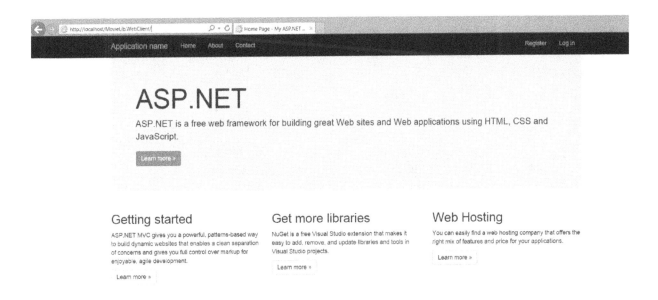

Pragmatic WCF

One more point to note here as well, you need console host running as this is hosting services. For this, you can set the console host application as the single startup file and keep running. Then, when you invoke the following URL http://localhost/MovieLib.WebClient/home/movielist , then it will hit the debugger as shown below.

```
string hostIdentity = WindowsIdentity.GetCurrent().Name;
string primary  hostIdentity  Q ▾ "AMERICAS\\Rahul_Sahay"  ⇦ ent.PrimaryIdentity.Name;
string windowsIdentity = ServiceSecurityContext.Current.WindowsIdentity.Name;
string threadIdentity = Thread.CurrentPrincipal.Identity.Name;
```

```
8 references   0/2 passing
public IEnumerable<MovieData> GetDirectorNames()
{

    string hostIdentity = WindowsIdentity.GetCurrent().Name;
    string primaryIdentity = ServiceSecurityContext.Current.PrimaryIdentity.Name;
    string windowsI  primaryIdentity  Q ▾ "IIS APPPOOL\\DefaultAppPool"  ⇦ wsIdentity.Name;
    string threadIdentity = Thread.CurrentPrincipal.Identity.Name;

    List<MovieData> movieData = new List<MovieData>();
```

Therefore, host identity is showing my name as windows authentication is set, other identities are showing IIS APPPOOL value as this is running as pass through setting. Here, you can also mimic browser call like a desktop call with soft impersonation. Below is the code for the same.

```
public ActionResult MovieList()
    {

        using (((WindowsIdentity)User.Identity).Impersonate())
        {

            proxyClient = new MovieClient("1stEP");

            proxyClient.Open();

            IEnumerable<MovieData> data = proxyClient.GetDirectorNames();

            proxyClient.Close();

        }

        return View();
```

Pragmatic WCF

```
    }
```

With the above changes in place, when I ran the same, it produced me the below result.

```
string hostIdentity = WindowsIdentity.GetCurrent().Name;
string primaryIdentity = ServiceSecurityContext.Current.PrimaryIdentity.Name;
string windowsIdenti  primaryIdentity  Q ▾ "AMERICAS\\Rahul_Sahay"  wsIdentity.Name;
string threadIdentity = Thread.CurrentPrincipal.Identity.Name;
```

INTERNET WEB APP:-

In Internet based security, little more configuration is required. On the binding side, we typically use **wsHttpBinding**. You can also use **basicHttpBinding**, which is by default unsecured binding. This is the only binding, which is by default unsecured. With **wsHttpBinding**, default security mode is set to **Message**, which is Transport in case of **tcpBinding.** In case of client credential type, we need to manually send user name and password. We need to create a token manually, not 100% manually, WCF will provide some help while doing so.

We also need to tell the service how it is going to negotiate with service credentials means is it going to use public key of certificate or is it going to have the public version of certificate in the client possession. Unlike TCP binding, HTTP binding is inherently unsecure, here tokens are sent as clear text. So, we do not have the protection level so that we can say protect this using Encrypt and Sign. In fact, we have to use certificate to protect the same. Once, these tokens reach at the service level, we can authenticate the same multiple ways. One of the ways are checking in windows domain if you have setup your box that way. Other way of doing the same is using ASP.NET provider for the same and write a custom solution for authenticating and authorizing the user.

Now, server side needs not only these binding configurations but also they need certificate information to be stored there as well. Client side also need some information to define the certificate trust level as if how is the client interact with certificate public key, is it going to be copy of the certificate without private key off course installed on the client machine. This is also known as **Peer Trust**.

- Peer Trust: - Client must have a copy of certificate without private key. Endpoint needs to define certificate name.

Pragmatic WCF

- Chain Trust: - Client must have encoded public key (base 64).

SECURITY MODE:-

When we are dealing with Internet based security and using HTTP binding, means we are dealing with clear text pipe. It is called message security and transport is not secure. We have to make sure that it is secured point to point. In order to do the same, we need to make sure that it is properly encrypted. We will get into the same little later, but first let us set the binding in console host app.config file. As you can see below, I have set the security mode to Message; hence, the inner tag, which we got here, is message. Here, also we got the option for client credential type, which we have set to username. One of settings, which I need to have with this, is set **NegotitateServiceCredential** to false. It means client is not excepted to have the physical copy of certificate containing public key. It also means by setting this to false, client is going to have the public key through some other mean.

```xml
<?xml version="1.0" encoding="utf-8"?>
<configuration>
  <configSections>
    <!-- For more information on Entity Framework configuration, visit http://go.microsoft.com/fwlink/?LinkID=237468 -->
    <section name="entityFramework" type="System.Data.Entity.Internal.ConfigFile.EntityFrameworkSection, EntityFramework, Version=6.0.0.0, Culture=neutral, PublicKeyToken=b77a5c561934e089" requirePermission="false" />
  </configSections>
  <startup>
    <supportedRuntime version="v4.0" sku=".NETFramework,Version=v4.5" />
  </startup>
  <entityFramework>
    <defaultConnectionFactory type="System.Data.Entity.Infrastructure.SqlConnectionFactory, EntityFramework" />
    <providers>
      <provider invariantName="System.Data.SqlClient" type="System.Data.Entity.SqlServer.SqlProviderServices, EntityFramework.SqlServer" />
    </providers>
  </entityFramework>
  <connectionStrings>
```

Pragmatic WCF

```xml
    <add name="MoviesReviewProd" connectionString="Data
Source=8133GTVZ1\SQLEXPRESS;Initial Catalog=MoviesReviewProd;Integrated Security=True"
providerName="System.Data.SqlClient" />

    </connectionStrings>
  <system.serviceModel>

    <services>

      <service name="MovieLib.Services.MovieManager">


        <endpoint address="net.tcp://localhost:8010/MovieService"

                binding="netTcpBinding" bindingConfiguration="tcpSecurity"

                contract="MovieLib.Contracts.IMovieService" />

        <endpoint address="http://localhost/MovieService"

                binding="wsHttpBinding"

                contract="MovieLib.Contracts.IMovieService"
bindingConfiguration="wsSecurity"/>

      </service>

    </services>

    <bindings>

      <netTcpBinding>

        <binding name="tcpSecurity">

          <security mode="Transport">

            <transport clientCredentialType="Windows" protectionLevel="Sign"/>

          </security>

        </binding>

      </netTcpBinding>

      <wsHttpBinding>

        <binding name="wsSecurity">

          <security mode="Message">
<message clientCredentialType="UserName" negotiateServiceCredential="false"/>
</security>

        </binding>

      </wsHttpBinding>

    </bindings>

  </system.serviceModel>

</configuration>
```

Pragmatic WCF

Now, let us go ahead and copy the bindings there in the client config file as well.

```xml
<?xml version="1.0" encoding="utf-8" ?>
<configuration>
  <startup>
    <supportedRuntime version="v4.0" sku=".NETFramework,Version=v4.5" />
  </startup>
  <system.serviceModel>
    <bindings>
      <basicHttpBinding>
        <binding name="BasicHttpBinding_IMovieService" />
      </basicHttpBinding>
      <netTcpBinding>
        <binding name="tcpSecurity" >
          <security mode="Transport">
            <transport clientCredentialType="Windows" protectionLevel="Sign"/>
          </security>
        </binding>
      </netTcpBinding>
      <wsHttpBinding>
        <binding name="wsSecurity">
          <security mode="Message">
            <message clientCredentialType="UserName" negotiateServiceCredential="false"/>
          </security>
        </binding>
      </wsHttpBinding>
    </bindings>
    <client>
      <endpoint address="net.tcp://localhost:8010/MovieService" binding="netTcpBinding"
        contract="MovieLib.Contracts.IMovieService" name="1stEP"
bindingConfiguration="tcpSecurity" />
      <endpoint address="http://localhost/MovieService" binding="wsHttpBinding"
        contract="MovieLib.Contracts.IMovieService" name="2ndEP"
bindingConfiguration="wsSecurity" />
      <endpoint address="net.tcp://localhost:8011/MovieName" binding="netTcpBinding"
```

Pragmatic WCF

```
        contract="MovieLib.Client.Contracts.IMovieName" />

    </client>

    </system.serviceModel>

</configuration>
```

SETTING BEHAVIOR:-

The identity, which I am going to show here, is the same and this is just the brief refresher. Now, when the service authenticates it can authenticate in one of the two ways. Client is already decided that it is going to use manual user name and password because the client may or may not be windows system. First way is service will accept the username and password and then build the windows token out of it and attempts to see if it is actually in the current windows store.

Moreover, we set this up in the app.config of service in the behavior section. Client does not know about this. Here, the settings we want is **ServiceCredentials**. This is also the place where, we are going to configure the certificate setting, which the service is going to find. However, we will do that little later. First, I am going to add the **userNameAuthentication** tag, which is going to tell the service how it is going to authenticate the incoming username. Now, here we can also set authorization. Outside the service Credentials, we can set **ServiceAuthorization**. So, in a nutshell, even though we are sending manual user name and password, service is taking them generating a windows token out of that and then authenticating the same in windows store. Below is the modified configuration for the same.

```
<system.serviceModel>

    <services>

    <service name="MovieLib.Services.MovieManager">

        <!--<host>

        <endpoint address="net.tcp://localhost:8010/MovieService"
                binding="netTcpBinding" bindingConfiguration="tcpSecurity"
                contract="MovieLib.Contracts.IMovieService" />
        <endpoint address="http://localhost/MovieService"
                binding="wsHttpBinding"
                contract="MovieLib.Contracts.IMovieService"
bindingConfiguration="wsSecurity"/>
```

Pragmatic WCF

```xml
        </service>
    </services>
    <bindings>
      <netTcpBinding>
        <binding name="tcpSecurity">
          <security mode="Transport">
            <transport clientCredentialType="Windows" protectionLevel="Sign"/>
          </security>
        </binding>
      </netTcpBinding>
      <wsHttpBinding>
        <binding name="wsSecurity">
          <security mode="Message">
            <message clientCredentialType="UserName" negotiateServiceCredential="false"/>
          </security>
        </binding>
      </wsHttpBinding>
    </bindings>
    <behaviors>
      <serviceBehaviors>
        <behavior>
          <serviceCredentials>
            <userNameAuthentication userNamePasswordValidationMode="Windows"/>
          </serviceCredentials>
          <serviceAuthorization principalPermissionMode="UseWindowsGroups"/>
        </behavior>
      </serviceBehaviors>
    </behaviors>
  </system.serviceModel>
```

We are not quite ready to run the same. If we run it, host will blow up because this is HTTP security without a certificate. We need to define the certificate for the same.

Pragmatic WCF

CERTIFICATE CREATION:-

Since, we are using clear pipe with HTTP, we need to encrypt these contents from prying eyes and the best way to do the same is using certificates. Now, the certificate, which we are going to create here, is **x.509** certificate. Below, I have pasted the script for creating the certificate.

makecert.exe -sr LocalMachine -ss Root -pe -sky exchange -n "CN=PragmaticWCF" PragmaticWCF.cer

pause

Now, let me tell you few things about the individual nomenclatures used here. Although I am not certificate expert. Nevertheless, let me give you brief idea on the same. Here, I am running **MakeCert.exe**, which is a windows utility; you need to run the same with elevated permission or an administrator. First, I am creating the certificate in my Local machine, in the root location. The name of the certificate is **PragmaticWCF** and file on which the certificate will be written is also **PragmaticWCF.**

Name	Date modified	Type	Size
MovieLib	5/31/2015 7:28 PM	File folder	
CreateCert	6/6/2015 12:13 PM	Windows Comma...	1 KB
makecert	9/27/2007 7:17 PM	Application	57 KB

Or you can run the same simply from Visual Studio command prompt in admin mode as shown below.

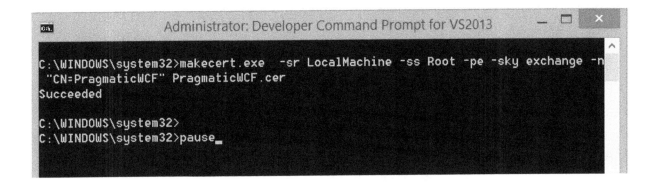

Pragmatic WCF

Once, the certificate successfully created, you can find the same in the root directory. You can navigate the same from management console. I have also pasted the management console shortcut here in the project folder.

MovieLib	5/31/2015 7:28 PM	File folder		
Certs	2/6/2015 4:46 AM	Microsoft Commo...		40 KB
CreateCert	6/6/2015 12:13 PM	Windows Comma...		1 KB
makecert	9/27/2007 7:17 PM	Application		57 KB

Once, you open the same, you can then see the certificate which was created here.

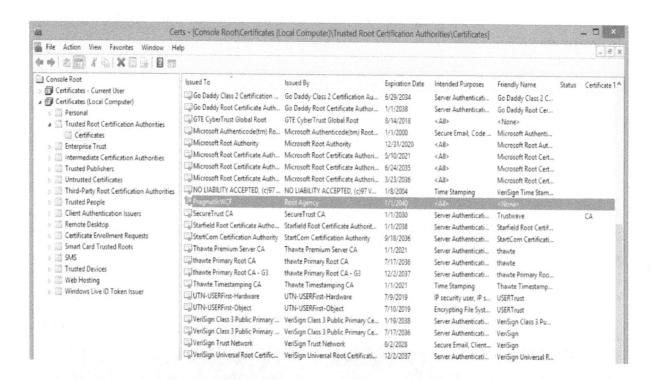

Therefore, as you can see in the above screen shot, there is a little key associated with the certificate, which says that it has the private key. Now, I need to take the certificate information and tell the config about it because host is going to reconcile the same with the contents of the certificate.

Pragmatic WCF

CONFIGURING CERTIFICATE:-

Below are the changes, which we need to do on the service side for accommodating the certificate. Now, let me go ahead and explain the code a bit. First setting is the store location, like where to look for this certificate.

```
<serviceBehaviors>
  <behavior>
    <serviceCredentials>
      <userNameAuthentication userNamePas  📄 CurrentUser          de="Windows"/>
      <serviceCertificate storeLocation="" 📄 LocalMachine         />

    </serviceCredentials>
    <serviceAuthorization principalPermissionMode="UseWindowsGroups"/>
  </behavior>
```

Then the next one is which store need to be referred. Then, the name of the certificate, which is nothing but telling WCF to look for this specific certificate. Then I have specified certificate type, which says, WCF will look for the type 509 certificate. Below is the setting in its finished form.

```
          </security>
        </binding>
      </wsHttpBinding>              📄 AddressBook
    </bindings>                    📄 AuthRoot
    <behaviors>                    📄 CertificateAuthority
      <serviceBehaviors>           📄 Disallowed
        <behavior>                 📄 My
          <serviceCredentials>     📄 Root
            <userNameAuthentication userNam 📄 TrustedPeople       de="Windows"/>
            <serviceCertificate storeLocati 📄 TrustedPublisher
                        storeName=""/>

          </serviceCredentials>



<system.serviceModel>

  <services>

    <service name="MovieLib.Services.MovieManager">

      <!--<host>

        <baseAddresses>
```

Pragmatic WCF

```xml
          <add baseAddress="http://localhost:8012"/>
          <add baseAddress="net.tcp://localhost:8010/MovieService"/>
        </baseAddresses>
      </host>-->


      <endpoint address="net.tcp://localhost:8010/MovieService"
              binding="netTcpBinding" bindingConfiguration="tcpSecurity"
              contract="MovieLib.Contracts.IMovieService" />
      <endpoint address="http://localhost/MovieService"
              binding="wsHttpBinding"
              contract="MovieLib.Contracts.IMovieService"
bindingConfiguration="wsSecurity"/>
      <!--<endpoint address="MEX"
              binding="mexTcpBinding"
              contract="IMetadataExchange"/>-->
    </service>
  </services>
  <bindings>
    <netTcpBinding>
      <binding name="tcpSecurity">
        <security mode="Transport">
          <transport clientCredentialType="Windows" protectionLevel="Sign"/>
        </security>
      </binding>
    </netTcpBinding>
    <wsHttpBinding>
      <binding name="wsSecurity">
        <security mode="Message">
          <message clientCredentialType="UserName" negotiateServiceCredential="false"/>
        </security>
      </binding>
    </wsHttpBinding>
  </bindings>
  <behaviors>
    <serviceBehaviors>
      <behavior>
```

Pragmatic WCF

```xml
        <serviceCredentials>
          <userNameAuthentication userNamePasswordValidationMode="Windows"/>
          <serviceCertificate storeLocation="LocalMachine"
                              storeName="Root"
                              findValue="PragmaticWCF"
                              x509FindType="FindBySubjectName"/>
        </serviceCredentials>
        <serviceAuthorization principalPermissionMode="UseWindowsGroups"/>
      </behavior>
    </serviceBehaviors>
  </behaviors>
</system.serviceModel>
```

Now, at this stage, I can check my host at least whether everything is done correctly or not. So, as you can see in the below screenshot, host is running as expected.

CLIENT CONFIGURATION:-

In this section, we are going to setup behavior at the client side as well. I have already told that behavior is all about service side, no client side intervention here. However, there is one behavior known as endpoint behavior, which is set at the client side. This is used to provide behavior characteristics to a particular endpoint and how it is going to make a call to the service. Below I have pasted the configs file for the client section.

```xml
<?xml version="1.0" encoding="utf-8" ?>
<configuration>
  <startup>
```

Pragmatic WCF

```xml
      <supportedRuntime version="v4.0" sku=".NETFramework,Version=v4.5" />
  </startup>
  <system.serviceModel>
    <bindings>
      <basicHttpBinding>
        <binding name="BasicHttpBinding_IMovieService" />
      </basicHttpBinding>
      <netTcpBinding>
        <binding name="tcpSecurity" >
          <security mode="Transport">
            <transport clientCredentialType="Windows" protectionLevel="Sign"/>
          </security>
        </binding>
      </netTcpBinding>
      <wsHttpBinding>
        <binding name="wsSecurity">
          <security mode="Message">
            <message clientCredentialType="UserName" negotiateServiceCredential="false"/>
          </security>
        </binding>
      </wsHttpBinding>
    </bindings>
    <behaviors>
      <endpointBehaviors>
        <behavior name="wsBehavior">
          <clientCredentials>
            <serviceCertificate>
              <authentication certificateValidationMode="ChainTrust"/>
            </serviceCertificate>
          </clientCredentials>
        </behavior>
      </endpointBehaviors>
    </behaviors>
    <client>
      <endpoint address="net.tcp://localhost:8010/MovieService" binding="netTcpBinding"
```

Pragmatic WCF

```
        contract="MovieLib.Contracts.IMovieService" name="1stEP"
bindingConfiguration="tcpSecurity" />

    <endpoint address="http://localhost/MovieService" binding="wsHttpBinding"

        contract="MovieLib.Contracts.IMovieService" name="2ndEP"
bindingConfiguration="wsSecurity" behaviorConfiguration="wsBehavior" />

    <endpoint address="net.tcp://localhost:8011/MovieName" binding="netTcpBinding"

        contract="MovieLib.Client.Contracts.IMovieName" />

    </client>

    </system.serviceModel>

</configuration>
```

Now, let me explain the code a bit. As you can see here, I have added endpoint behavior here and referenced the same in the WS HTTP Binding section. In addition, in the behavior section, I am actually telling the client how it will obtain the public key information for the certificate. First, I added the client credential section and then I added Service certificate section where I have added the validation mode and set this to **Chain Trust**. As I mentioned during the beginning of this chapter, that client will obtain the public key information right here in the config and the service certificate can be found in the root store. Hence, now we have to give the client information about the public key.

We need to create a file that will contain the public key of the certificate. In order to achieve the same, we need to go into the management console and follow the below steps.

Pragmatic WCF

Issued To	Issued By	Expiration Date
Go Daddy Class 2 Certification ...	Go Daddy Class 2 Certification Au...	6/29/2034
Go Daddy Root Certificate Auth...	Go Daddy Root Certificate Author...	1/1/2038
GTE CyberTrust Global Root	GTE CyberTrust Global Root	8/14/2018
Microsoft Authenticode(tm) Ro...	Microsoft Authenticode(tm) Root...	1/1/2000
Microsoft Root Authority	Microsoft Root Authority	12/31/2020
Microsoft Root Certificate Auth...	Microsoft Root Certificate Authori...	5/10/2021
Microsoft Root Certificate Auth...	Microsoft Root Certificate Authori...	6/24/2035
Microsoft Root Certificate Auth...	Microsoft Root Certificate Authori...	3/23/2036
NO LIABILITY ACCEPTED, (c)97 ...	NO LIABILITY ACCEPTED, (c)97 V...	1/8/2004
PragmaticWCF	Root ...	1/1/2040
SecureTrust CA	Secu	1/1/2030
Starfield Root Certificate Autho...	Star	
StartCom Certification Authority	Star	
Thawte Premium Server CA	Tha	
thawte Primary Root CA	thav	7/17/2036
thawte Primary Root CA - G3	thav	12/2/2037
Thawte Timestamping CA	Tha	1/1/2021
UTN-USERFirst-Hardware	UTN	7/9/2019
UTN-USERFirst-Object	UTN	7/10/2019
VeriSign Class 3 Public Primary ...	VeriSign Class 3 Public Primary Ce...	1/19/2038

Context menu overlay:
- Open
- All Tasks ▶
  - Open
  - Export...
- Cut
- Copy
- Delete
- Properties
- Help

Pragmatic WCF

Pragmatic WCF

Pragmatic WCF

Pragmatic WCF

Pragmatic WCF

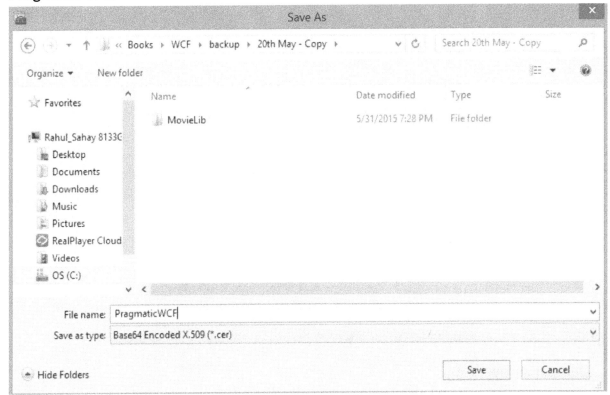

Pragmatic WCF

Then, upon clicking on Finish button, it will give the below confirmation message.

Pragmatic WCF

Therefore, now when I go in my directory, I can see the certificate was created with public key in it.

Name	Date modified	Type	Size
MovieLib	5/31/2015 7:28 PM	File folder	
Certs	6/6/2015 6:12 PM	Microsoft Commo...	40 KB
CreateCert	6/6/2015 12:13 PM	Windows Comma...	1 KB
makecert	9/27/2007 7:17 PM	Application	57 KB
PragmaticWCF	6/6/2015 6:10 PM	Security Certificate	1 KB

When I open the same in the notepad, it will open like shown below. As you see, it is readable and **base 64** encoded.

```
 1   -----BEGIN CERTIFICATE-----
 2   MIICODCCAeagAwIBAgIQst8hxxs+Na9Ly/zPtQGWXjAJBgUrDgMCHQUAMBYxFDAS
 3   BgNVBAMTC1Jvb3QgQWdlbmN5MB4XDTE1MDYwNjA3MDAyM1oXDTM5MTIzMTIzNTk1
 4   OVowFzEVMBMGA1UEAxMMUHJhZ21hdGljV0NGMIIBIjANBgkqhkiG9w0BAQEFAAOC
 5   AQ8AMIIBCgKCAQEA4V+HzPLZc71HeL5S/aoNHi0CATLR+n+t8BwQjP64tyb9iTQ1
 6   tnETd/yyQwbjKLO2pnNY/43CjdyLt9OnJZKxnvNeRxoOtMiCPc6MmdaLfwuT8Erc
 7   CHS33xvADx//HHUY1sV7QSuN+K1TTzq1TAzei65yd+VX4xqAC4pXCwwK4ASxjVl4
 8   DvsqfvE6D9Gh+dWwnDD8Des/gVvwT0w7oBd3GZencbhB3muBxntVjTycbMKWiv06
 9   PSFWuGwcJwbgVsvWU7a7V4iGRcGiX5ir3xktYu//spQ8IxfAH4liqHD0E6I1vrf1
10   S7LbK5/1QEEVgTB1lLLMaCjkYz9LsLkWuV3UNwIDAQABo0swSTBHBgNVHQEEQDA+
11   gBAS5AktBh0dTwCNYSHcFmRjoRgwFjEUMBIGA1UEAxMLUm9vdCBBZ2VuY3mCEAY3
12   bACqAGSKEc+41KpcNfQwCQYFKw4DAh0FAANBACLtNEUkz/ne1R0eDbzQHXOkVquX
13   MmhNU9QvSC9qW+eQnZRipn9uGHHbd0F1wv/EbkSdgE1prjqpwiZXWhdhqck=
14   -----END CERTIFICATE-----
15
```

Now, I will simply copy this value and put this in the endpoint section of the client config under encoded value as shown below.

```
<?xml version="1.0" encoding="utf-8" ?>
```

Pragmatic WCF

```
<configuration>
  <startup>
    <supportedRuntime version="v4.0" sku=".NETFramework,Version=v4.5" />
  </startup>
  <system.serviceModel>
    <bindings>
      <basicHttpBinding>
        <binding name="BasicHttpBinding_IMovieService" />
      </basicHttpBinding>
      <netTcpBinding>
        <binding name="tcpSecurity" >
          <security mode="Transport">
            <transport clientCredentialType="Windows" protectionLevel="Sign"/>
          </security>
        </binding>
      </netTcpBinding>
      <wsHttpBinding>
        <binding name="wsSecurity">
          <security mode="Message">
            <message clientCredentialType="UserName" negotiateServiceCredential="false"/>
          </security>
        </binding>
      </wsHttpBinding>
    </bindings>
    <behaviors>
      <endpointBehaviors>
        <behavior name="wsBehavior">
          <clientCredentials>
            <serviceCertificate>
              <authentication certificateValidationMode="ChainTrust"/>
            </serviceCertificate>
          </clientCredentials>
        </behavior>
      </endpointBehaviors>
    </behaviors>
    <client>
```

Pragmatic WCF

```
        <endpoint address="net.tcp://localhost:8010/MovieService" binding="netTcpBinding"
            contract="MovieLib.Contracts.IMovieService" name="1stEP"
bindingConfiguration="tcpSecurity" />

        <endpoint address="http://localhost/MovieService" binding="wsHttpBinding"
            contract="MovieLib.Contracts.IMovieService" name="2ndEP"
bindingConfiguration="wsSecurity" behaviorConfiguration="wsBehavior">

        <identity>

            <certificate
encodedValue="MIICODCCAeagAwIBAgIQst8hxxs+Na9Ly/zPtQGWXjAJBgUrDgMCHQUAMBYxFDAS

BgNVBAMTC1Jvb3QgQWdlbmN5MB4XDTE1MDYwNjA3MDAyM1oXDTM5MTIzMTIzNTk1

OVowFzEVMBMGA1UEAxMMUHJhZ21hdGljV0NGMIIBIjANBgkqhkiG9w0BAQEFAAOC

AQ8AMIIBCgKCAQEA4V+HzPLZc71HeL5S/aoNHi0CATLR+n+t8BwQjP64tyb9iTQ1

tnETd/yyQwbjKLO2pnNY/43CjdyLt9OnJZKxnvNeRxoOtMiCPc6MmdaLfwuT8Erc

CHS33xvADx//HHUY1sV7QSuN+K1TTzq1TAzei65yd+VX4xqAC4pXCwwK4ASxjVl4

DvsqfvE6D9Gh+dWwnDD8Des/gVvwT0w7oBd3GZencbhB3muBxntVjTycbMKWiv06

PSFWuGwcJwbgVsvWU7a7V4iGRcGiX5ir3xktYu//spQ8IxfAH4liqHD0E6I1vrf1

S7LbK5/lQEEVgTB1lLLMaCjkYz9LsLkWuV3UNwIDAQABo0swSTBHBgNVHQEEQDA+

gBAS5AktBh0dTwCNYSHcFmRjoRgwFjEUMBIGA1UEAxMLUm9vdCBBZ2VuY3mCEAY3

bACqAGSKEc+41KpcNfQwCQYFKw4DAh0FAANBACLtNEUkz/ne1R0eDbzQHXOkVquX

MmhNU9QvSC9qW+eQnZRipn9uGHHbd0F1wv/EbkSdgE1prjqpwiZXWhdhqck="/>

        </identity>

        </endpoint>

        <endpoint address="net.tcp://localhost:8011/MovieName" binding="netTcpBinding"
            contract="MovieLib.Client.Contracts.IMovieName" />

    </client>

  </system.serviceModel>

</configuration>
```

Now, I will go in the client code and set up the client credentials like this.

Pragmatic WCF

```csharp
1 reference
private async void Button_Click(object sender, RoutedEventArgs e)
{
    // MovieClient proxyClient = new MovieClient("1stEP");

    proxyClient.ClientCredentials.UserName.

    try
    {
        await Task.Run(() =>
        {
            IEnumerable<MovieData> data            etDirectorNames();
            if (data != null)
            {
                SendOrPostCallback callback = (arg =>
                {
                    LstDirectors.ItemsSource = data;
                });
                synchronizationContext.Send(callback, true);
            }

            //    proxyClient.Close();
        });
```

```
    Equals
    GetHashCode
    GetType
    Password
    ToString
    UserName
```

As you can see in the above screenshot, it has two properties Username and Password not the domain. Hence, we can give username and password and service will authenticate or tempt to authenticate the same.

```csharp
private async void Button_Click(object sender, RoutedEventArgs e)
{
    proxyClient.ClientCredentials.UserName.UserName = "dummyUser";
    proxyClient.ClientCredentials.UserName.Password = "dummyPassword";

    try
    {
        await Task.Run(() =>
        {
            IEnumerable<MovieData> data = proxyClient.GetDirectorNames();
            if (data != null)
            {
```

Pragmatic WCF

```
            SendOrPostCallback callback = (arg =>
            {
                LstDirectors.ItemsSource = data;
            });
            synchronizationContext.Send(callback, true);
        }


    });
```

Upon, running the same, it will produce you the desired output. One more thing is that

```
string hostIdentity = WindowsIdentity.GetCurrent().Name;
string primaryIdentity = ServiceSecurityContext.Current.PrimaryIdentity.Name;
string windowsIdenti[⊕ primaryIdentity  Q ▾ "AMERICAS\\dummyUser" ⊡ ]wsIdentity.Name;
string threadIdentity = Thread.CurrentPrincipal.Identity.Name;

List<MovieData> movieData = new List<MovieData>();
```

Other way of doing the same is via ASP.NET Providers where in you can create your custom
provider with username and roles associated with it.

ASP.NET PROVIDER:-

To provide a custom solution, WCF uses ASP.NET provider. It is the same pattern, which
introduced in ASP.NET 2.0. Microsoft also provider built in generator, which generates database
stuffs for you. Therefore, if you would like to do the same with Microsoft SQL Server or
Microsoft Role Provider, you can go ahead and do the same. Hence, without wasting time, I am

Pragmatic WCF

going to write my custom provider. As you can see below in the screen shot, I have created new folder for custom providers in my host solution. Moreover, here, I will add my first set of users'.

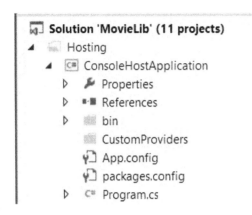

Here, I have added my Users class with following roles and users to it.

```csharp
using System.Collections.Generic;

namespace ConsoleHostApplication.CustomProviders
{
    public class Users : List<User>
    {
        public static Users Load()
        {
            Users users = new Users();

            users.Add(new User()
            {
                UserName = "rahul",
                Roles = new List<string>() { "user", "admin" }
            });
            users.Add(new User()
            {
                UserName = "nivi",
```

Pragmatic WCF

```
                Roles = new List<string>() { "user" }
        });
        users.Add(new User()
        {
            UserName = "aadi",
            Roles = new List<string>() { "user" }
        });

        return users;
    }
public User FindUser(string userName)
    {
        return Find(u => u.UserName == userName);
    }

}


public class User
{
    public string UserName { get; set; }
    public List<string> Roles { get; set; }
    public bool IsInRole(string role)
    {
        return Roles.Contains(role);
    }


}
}
```

Here I have just hardcoded the stuffs to give quick little demo. Now, I will go ahead and create custom membership provider say **MyMembershipProvider** that will be inherited from **MembershipProvider.** During creation, when I implemented the abstract class, it gave me bunch of membership related stuffs as shown below.

Pragmatic WCF

```
using System.Web.Security;


namespace ConsoleHostApplication.CustomProviders
{
    public abstract class MyMembershipProvider : MembershipProvider
    {
        public override string ApplicationName
        {
            get
            {
                throw new System.NotImplementedException();
            }
            set
            {
                throw new System.NotImplementedException();
            }
        }


        public override bool ChangePassword(string username, string oldPassword, string
newPassword)
        {
            throw new System.NotImplementedException();
        }


        public override bool ChangePasswordQuestionAndAnswer(string username, string
password, string newPasswordQuestion, string newPasswordAnswer)
        {
            throw new System.NotImplementedException();
        }


        public override MembershipUser CreateUser(string username, string password,
string email, string passwordQuestion, string passwordAnswer, bool isApproved, object
providerUserKey, out MembershipCreateStatus status)
        {
            throw new System.NotImplementedException();
        }
```

Pragmatic WCF

```csharp
        public override bool DeleteUser(string username, bool deleteAllRelatedData)
        {
            throw new System.NotImplementedException();
        }


        public override bool EnablePasswordReset
        {
            get { throw new System.NotImplementedException(); }
        }


        public override bool EnablePasswordRetrieval
        {
            get { throw new System.NotImplementedException(); }
        }


        public override MembershipUserCollection FindUsersByEmail(string emailToMatch,
int pageIndex, int pageSize, out int totalRecords)
        {
            throw new System.NotImplementedException();
        }


        public override MembershipUserCollection FindUsersByName(string usernameToMatch,
int pageIndex, int pageSize, out int totalRecords)
        {
            throw new System.NotImplementedException();
        }


        public override MembershipUserCollection GetAllUsers(int pageIndex, int pageSize,
out int totalRecords)
        {
            throw new System.NotImplementedException();
        }


        public override int GetNumberOfUsersOnline()
        {
            throw new System.NotImplementedException();
        }
```

Pragmatic WCF

```
public override string GetPassword(string username, string answer)
{
    throw new System.NotImplementedException();
}


public override MembershipUser GetUser(string username, bool userIsOnline)
{
    throw new System.NotImplementedException();
}


public override MembershipUser GetUser(object providerUserKey, bool userIsOnline)
{
    throw new System.NotImplementedException();
}


public override string GetUserNameByEmail(string email)
{
    throw new System.NotImplementedException();
}


public override int MaxInvalidPasswordAttempts
{
    get { throw new System.NotImplementedException(); }
}


public override int MinRequiredNonAlphanumericCharacters
{
    get { throw new System.NotImplementedException(); }
}


public override int MinRequiredPasswordLength
{
    get { throw new System.NotImplementedException(); }
}
```

Pragmatic WCF

```
    public override int PasswordAttemptWindow

    {

        get { throw new System.NotImplementedException(); }

    }


    public override MembershipPasswordFormat PasswordFormat

    {

        get { throw new System.NotImplementedException(); }

    }


    public override string PasswordStrengthRegularExpression

    {

        get { throw new System.NotImplementedException(); }

    }


    public override bool RequiresQuestionAndAnswer

    {

        get { throw new System.NotImplementedException(); }

    }


    public override bool RequiresUniqueEmail

    {

        get { throw new System.NotImplementedException(); }

    }


    public override string ResetPassword(string username, string answer)

    {

        throw new System.NotImplementedException();

    }


    public override bool UnlockUser(string userName)

    {

        throw new System.NotImplementedException();

    }


    public override void UpdateUser(MembershipUser user)
```

Pragmatic WCF

```
        {
            throw new System.NotImplementedException();
        }


        public override bool ValidateUser(string username, string password)
        {
            throw new System.NotImplementedException();
        }
    }
}
```

But, for our custom implementation, we don't need any of them except one validate user. And, in Validate User, I am going to load my users' list which I have created and return whether user exists or not.

```
using System.Collections.Specialized;
using System.Web.Security;

namespace ConsoleHostApplication.CustomProviders
{
    public class MyMembershipProvider : MembershipProvider
    {
        private string _connectionString = "";
        public override void Initialize(string name, NameValueCollection config)
        {
            _connectionString = config["connectionString"];
            base.Initialize(_connectionString,config);
        }


        public override bool ValidateUser(string username, string password)
        {
            Users users = Users.Load();
            return (users.FindUser(username) != null);
        }
```

Pragmatic WCF

```csharp
public override string ApplicationName
{
    get
    {
        throw new System.NotImplementedException();
    }
    set
    {
        throw new System.NotImplementedException();
    }
}


public override bool ChangePassword(string username, string oldPassword, string newPassword)
{
    throw new System.NotImplementedException();
}


public override bool ChangePasswordQuestionAndAnswer(string username, string password, string newPasswordQuestion, string newPasswordAnswer)
{
    throw new System.NotImplementedException();
}


public override MembershipUser CreateUser(string username, string password, string email, string passwordQuestion, string passwordAnswer, bool isApproved, object providerUserKey, out MembershipCreateStatus status)
{
    throw new System.NotImplementedException();
}


public override bool DeleteUser(string username, bool deleteAllRelatedData)
{
    throw new System.NotImplementedException();
}
```

Pragmatic WCF

```csharp
        public override bool EnablePasswordReset
        {
            get { throw new System.NotImplementedException(); }
        }


        public override bool EnablePasswordRetrieval
        {
            get { throw new System.NotImplementedException(); }
        }


        public override MembershipUserCollection FindUsersByEmail(string emailToMatch,
int pageIndex, int pageSize, out int totalRecords)
        {
            throw new System.NotImplementedException();
        }


        public override MembershipUserCollection FindUsersByName(string usernameToMatch,
int pageIndex, int pageSize, out int totalRecords)
        {
            throw new System.NotImplementedException();
        }


        public override MembershipUserCollection GetAllUsers(int pageIndex, int pageSize,
out int totalRecords)
        {
            throw new System.NotImplementedException();
        }


        public override int GetNumberOfUsersOnline()
        {
            throw new System.NotImplementedException();
        }


        public override string GetPassword(string username, string answer)
        {
            throw new System.NotImplementedException();
        }
```

Pragmatic WCF

```csharp
public override MembershipUser GetUser(string username, bool userIsOnline)
{
    throw new System.NotImplementedException();
}


public override MembershipUser GetUser(object providerUserKey, bool userIsOnline)
{
    throw new System.NotImplementedException();
}


public override string GetUserNameByEmail(string email)
{
    throw new System.NotImplementedException();
}


public override int MaxInvalidPasswordAttempts
{
    get { throw new System.NotImplementedException(); }
}


public override int MinRequiredNonAlphanumericCharacters
{
    get { throw new System.NotImplementedException(); }
}


public override int MinRequiredPasswordLength
{
    get { throw new System.NotImplementedException(); }
}


public override int PasswordAttemptWindow
{
    get { throw new System.NotImplementedException(); }
}
```

Pragmatic WCF

```
public override MembershipPasswordFormat PasswordFormat
{
    get { throw new System.NotImplementedException(); }
}


public override string PasswordStrengthRegularExpression
{
    get { throw new System.NotImplementedException(); }
}


public override bool RequiresQuestionAndAnswer
{
    get { throw new System.NotImplementedException(); }
}


public override bool RequiresUniqueEmail
{
    get { throw new System.NotImplementedException(); }
}


public override string ResetPassword(string username, string answer)
{
    throw new System.NotImplementedException();
}


public override bool UnlockUser(string userName)
{
    throw new System.NotImplementedException();
}


public override void UpdateUser(MembershipUser user)
{
    throw new System.NotImplementedException();
}
    }
}
```

Pragmatic WCF

However, here we need to put little configuration item as well. In order to do the same, you can simply go ahead and override the initialize piece as shown below.

```csharp
using System.Collections.Specialized;
using System.Web.Security;

namespace ConsoleHostApplication.CustomProviders
{
    public abstract class MyMembershipProvider : MembershipProvider
    {
        private string _connectionString = "";
        public override void Initialize(string name, NameValueCollection config)
        {
            _connectionString = config["connectionString"];
             base.Initialize(_connectionString,config);
        }

        public override bool ValidateUser(string username, string password)
        {
            Users users = Users.Load();
            return (users.FindUser(username) != null);
        }
    }
}
```

Now, I will go ahead and put the provider code in the config section as shown below.

```xml
<?xml version="1.0" encoding="utf-8"?>
<configuration>
  <configSections>
```

Pragmatic WCF

```xml
    <!-- For more information on Entity Framework configuration, visit
http://go.microsoft.com/fwlink/?LinkID=237468 -->

    <section name="entityFramework"
type="System.Data.Entity.Internal.ConfigFile.EntityFrameworkSection, EntityFramework,
Version=6.0.0.0, Culture=neutral, PublicKeyToken=b77a5c561934e089"
requirePermission="false" />

  </configSections>

  <startup>

    <supportedRuntime version="v4.0" sku=".NETFramework,Version=v4.5" />

  </startup>

  <entityFramework>

    <defaultConnectionFactory
type="System.Data.Entity.Infrastructure.SqlConnectionFactory, EntityFramework" />

    <providers>

      <provider invariantName="System.Data.SqlClient"
type="System.Data.Entity.SqlServer.SqlProviderServices, EntityFramework.SqlServer" />

    </providers>

  </entityFramework>

  <connectionStrings>

    <add name="MoviesReviewProd" connectionString="Data
Source=8133GTVZ1\SQLEXPRESS;Initial Catalog=MoviesReviewProd;Integrated Security=True"
providerName="System.Data.SqlClient" />

  </connectionStrings>

  <system.serviceModel>

    <services>

      <service name="MovieLib.Services.MovieManager">


        <endpoint address="net.tcp://localhost:8010/MovieService"

                binding="netTcpBinding" bindingConfiguration="tcpSecurity"

                contract="MovieLib.Contracts.IMovieService" />

        <endpoint address="http://localhost/MovieService"

                binding="wsHttpBinding"

                contract="MovieLib.Contracts.IMovieService"
bindingConfiguration="wsSecurity"/>

      </service>

    </services>

    <bindings>

      <netTcpBinding>
```

Pragmatic WCF

```xml
          <binding name="tcpSecurity">
            <security mode="Transport">
              <transport clientCredentialType="Windows" protectionLevel="Sign"/>
            </security>
          </binding>
        </netTcpBinding>
        <wsHttpBinding>
          <binding name="wsSecurity">
            <security mode="Message">
              <message clientCredentialType="UserName" negotiateServiceCredential="false"/>
            </security>
          </binding>
        </wsHttpBinding>
      </bindings>
      <behaviors>
        <serviceBehaviors>
          <behavior>
            <serviceCredentials>
              <userNameAuthentication userNamePasswordValidationMode="MembershipProvider"
membershipProviderName="myProvider"/>
              <serviceCertificate storeLocation="LocalMachine"
                                  storeName="Root"
                                  findValue="PragmaticWCF"
                                  x509FindType="FindBySubjectName"/>
            </serviceCredentials>
            <serviceAuthorization principalPermissionMode="UseWindowsGroups"/>
          </behavior>
        </serviceBehaviors>
      </behaviors>
    </system.serviceModel>
    <system.web>
      <membership>
        <providers>
          <add name="myProvider"
type="ConsoleHostApplication.CustomProviders,ConsoleHostApplication"
connectionString="MyConnection"/>
        </providers>
```

Pragmatic WCF

```
    </membership>
  </system.web>
</configuration>
```

Let me explain the stuffs, which I have changed here. First thing is, I have included the provider section where in I have included my custom provider with fully qualified namespace and assembly name. Second important thing is I have also included the **connectionString** as argument here. This means when membership provider will get initialized, its name value pair will have all these values. Then I have also changed the user name authentication attribute to membership provider rather windows. This also means that I have to provide the membership provider name here as well. So, this is how you point from WCF to a specific provider.

Now, let me go ahead and add another file for Role provider. Below is the snippet for the same. This is checking what role user is having.

```
using System.Web.Security;

namespace ConsoleHostApplication.CustomProviders
{
    public class MyRoleProvider : RoleProvider
    {
        public override bool IsUserInRole(string username, string roleName)
        {
            User user = Users.Load().FindUser(username);
            return user.IsInRole(roleName);
        }


        public override void AddUsersToRoles(string[] usernames, string[] roleNames)
        {
            throw new System.NotImplementedException();
        }
```

Pragmatic WCF

```csharp
    public override string ApplicationName
    {
        get
        {
            throw new System.NotImplementedException();
        }
        set
        {
            throw new System.NotImplementedException();
        }
    }


    public override void CreateRole(string roleName)
    {
        throw new System.NotImplementedException();
    }


    public override bool DeleteRole(string roleName, bool throwOnPopulatedRole)
    {
        throw new System.NotImplementedException();
    }


    public override string[] FindUsersInRole(string roleName, string usernameToMatch)
    {
        throw new System.NotImplementedException();
    }


    public override string[] GetAllRoles()
    {
        throw new System.NotImplementedException();
    }


    public override string[] GetRolesForUser(string username)
    {
        throw new System.NotImplementedException();
    }
```

Pragmatic WCF

```csharp
public override string[] GetUsersInRole(string roleName)
{
    throw new System.NotImplementedException();
}


public override void RemoveUsersFromRoles(string[] usernames, string[] roleNames)
{
    throw new System.NotImplementedException();
}


public override bool RoleExists(string roleName)
{
    throw new System.NotImplementedException();
}

    }
}
```

Once, this is done, let us configure the config file for using roles.

```xml
<?xml version="1.0" encoding="utf-8"?>
<configuration>
  <configSections>
    <!-- For more information on Entity Framework configuration, visit
http://go.microsoft.com/fwlink/?LinkID=237468 -->
    <section name="entityFramework"
type="System.Data.Entity.Internal.ConfigFile.EntityFrameworkSection, EntityFramework,
Version=6.0.0.0, Culture=neutral, PublicKeyToken=b77a5c561934e089"
requirePermission="false" />
  </configSections>
  <startup>
    <supportedRuntime version="v4.0" sku=".NETFramework,Version=v4.5" />
  </startup>
  <entityFramework>
    <defaultConnectionFactory
type="System.Data.Entity.Infrastructure.SqlConnectionFactory, EntityFramework" />
```

Pragmatic WCF

```
    <providers>
        <provider invariantName="System.Data.SqlClient"
type="System.Data.Entity.SqlServer.SqlProviderServices, EntityFramework.SqlServer" />
    </providers>
  </entityFramework>
  <connectionStrings>
    <add name="MoviesReviewProd" connectionString="Data
Source=8133GTVZ1\SQLEXPRESS;Initial Catalog=MoviesReviewProd;Integrated Security=True"
providerName="System.Data.SqlClient" />
  </connectionStrings>
  <system.serviceModel>
    <services>
      <service name="MovieLib.Services.MovieManager">


        <endpoint address="net.tcp://localhost:8010/MovieService"
                binding="netTcpBinding" bindingConfiguration="tcpSecurity"
                contract="MovieLib.Contracts.IMovieService" />
        <endpoint address="http://localhost/MovieService"
                binding="wsHttpBinding"
                contract="MovieLib.Contracts.IMovieService"
bindingConfiguration="wsSecurity"/>
      </service>
    </services>
    <bindings>
      <netTcpBinding>
        <binding name="tcpSecurity">
          <security mode="Transport">
            <transport clientCredentialType="Windows" protectionLevel="Sign"/>
          </security>
        </binding>
      </netTcpBinding>
      <wsHttpBinding>
        <binding name="wsSecurity">
          <security mode="Message">
            <message clientCredentialType="UserName" negotiateServiceCredential="false"/>
          </security>
        </binding>
```

Pragmatic WCF

```xml
        </wsHttpBinding>

    </bindings>

    <behaviors>

      <serviceBehaviors>

        <behavior>

          <serviceCredentials>

            <userNameAuthentication userNamePasswordValidationMode="MembershipProvider"
membershipProviderName="myProvider"/>

            <serviceCertificate storeLocation="LocalMachine"

                                storeName="Root"

                                findValue="PragmaticWCF"

                                x509FindType="FindBySubjectName"/>

          </serviceCredentials>

          <serviceAuthorization principalPermissionMode="UseAspNetRoles"
roleProviderName="myProvider"/>

        </behavior>

      </serviceBehaviors>

    </behaviors>

  </system.serviceModel>

  <system.web>

    <membership>

      <providers>

        <add name="myProvider" type="
ConsoleHostApplication.CustomProviders.MyMembershipProvider,ConsoleHostApplication"
connectionString="MyConnection"/>

      </providers>

    </membership>

    <roleManager enabled="true">

      <providers>

        <add name="myProvider" type="
ConsoleHostApplication.CustomProviders.MyRoleProvider,ConsoleHostApplication "/>

      </providers>

    </roleManager>

  </system.web>

</configuration>
```

Pragmatic WCF

Here, I have done couple of things like added role provider section and added fully qualified type to it, and then I have changed the Service Authorization mode to **UseAspNetRoles**. With the above change in place, when I go ahead and run the app, it will give me argument value as configured in configs file as shown below.

```
I reference
public override void Initialize(string name, NameValueCollection config)
{
    _connectionString = config["connectionString"];
    base.Initialize  _connectionString  Q ▾ "MyConnection"
}
```

Therefore, here it produced my identity after passing the username as rahul.

```
8 references   0/2 passing
public IEnumerable<MovieData> GetDirectorNames()
{
    string hostIdentity = WindowsIdentity.GetCurrent().Name;
    string primaryIdentity = ServiceSecurityContext.Current.PrimaryIdentity.Name;
    string windowsIdenti  primaryIdentity  Q ▾ "rahul"  .Current.WindowsIdentity.Name;
    string threadIdentity = Thread.CurrentPrincipal.Identity.Name;

    List<MovieData> movieData = new List<MovieData>();
```

With this, I would like to finish this chapter and this course as well.

SUMMARY:-

In this section, we have seen bunch of security related scenarios. We started with basic understanding and then delved each scenario with complete detail. We have seen how authentication works; how authorization works. Then, we covered demos for each of them. We also covered different types of security modes and its implementation. Last but not the least we have covered both intranet and internet security scenarios. I hope you have enjoyed the book.

Pragmatic WCF

About the Author

Rahul Sahay is a software developer living in Bangalore, India. Rahul has been working in various aspects of the software development life cycle since 7.5 years, focusing on Microsoft technology-specific development. He has been part of the development in different applications, ranging from client applications to web services to websites.

Rahul is a Senior Consultant at **Capgemini**. But he works for Capgemini's client **Dell R&D**, on their premier e-commerce portal ("*http://www.dell.com/account*"). His roles and responsibilities at this project are very tech-oriented like analyzing existing use cases and taking the new requirements to add features on the existing segment. Prior to Capgemini, he has been associated with **Mindtree** and **TCS**. He is also an active blogger; his writings can be viewed at *http://myview.rahulnivi.net/*. You can also refer his professional profile @ *http://in.linkedin.com/in/rahulsahay19.* Alternatively, follow him at twitter "*@rahulsahay19*".

He has also authored couple of books on MVC **Hands-On with ASP.NET MVC and Angular using MVC, Web API**; written completely right from the scratch with live demo by hosting the same on azure. You can refer this book at this URL http://ow.ly/JetAi & http://amzn.to/1w9sllt

Pragmatic WCF

Pragmatic WCF

Pragmatic WCF

Pragmatic WCF